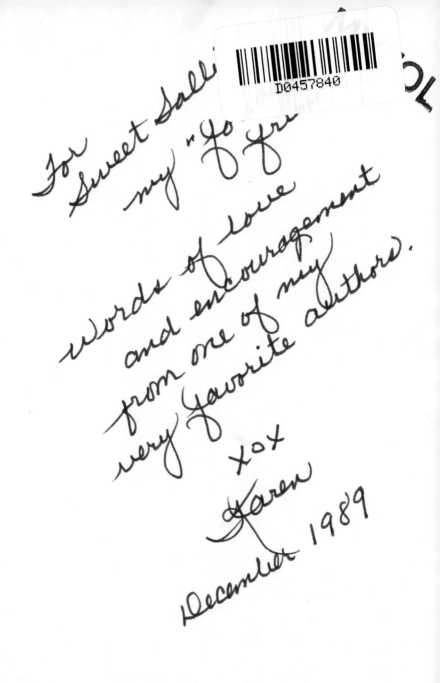

For
Sweet Sally
my "To girl"
words of love
and encouragement
from one of my
very favorite authors.

xox
Karen
December 1989

Of Time and Eternity

A Collection of the Writings of
James Dillet Freeman

UNITY BOOKS
Unity Village, Missouri

Second Printing, 1985

Cover photo: Lake Como Castle, Italy
By Tony La Tona

All Bible quotations
are from the King James Version
unless otherwise noted.

CONTENTS

About the Book

This is a collection of some of my writings that have never before appeared in a book. I have been writing for Unity for almost fifty years; hundreds of pieces written by me have appeared in Unity publications and elsewhere. I have chosen these in the hope that they will help you answer some of your questions and meet some of your needs—and mainly because I like them.

The pieces have come to me in different ways at different times. Writing for me is a kind of prayer. I ask God if He has anything to tell me that is true about Him and the world and you and me and life—or that may be helpful to someone—and I ask Him to help me to put down what comes as simply and vividly as I can.

I have always had a strong feeling about my writing—at its best I don't write it, it comes to me, though sometimes only after hard work. Usually it is not an extended piece that comes, but only bursts and snatches, and it takes work to bring it to completion. But I am grateful for any momentary flare of inspiration. For I feel that I have been vouchsafed an occasional glimpse into the nature of things and have come upon a few useful truths. And it is a special joy when what comes to me clothes itself—as fortunately it sometimes does—in words that are not only simple and clear but make a kind of music; for then I know that those who read it may not only see the truth with their minds but feel it in their hearts.

For instance, I was sitting at my desk one morning, thinking about I know not what, when suddenly I found myself writing the seven sentences that conclude "The Evolution of the God-Idea." Turning these sentences into the full essay that is in this book took time and effort; but as these words sang themselves into my head, you can imagine my delight. I no sooner had them down than I rushed off to read them to my wife and anyone else who would listen. Reading them still thrills me, for they contain a great truth.

At another time, a person who had gotten into a great deal of trouble doing something that made him feel very guilty came to me for counsel and prayer. The next morning while he was out performing his wicked act, I was praying for him, and my prayer shaped itself into "Because He Is Love."

I was catching a quick lunch with my wife in a fast food restaurant when I had "A Conversation with a Mayfly." Sir Dalliance O'Day wafted down upon the window that was beside our table and began his elucidation of the nature of things.

I had been laboring all of a summer morning on a piece about health that I was not happy with. That afternoon I went out on my patio to relax in the warm sunlight and an altogether different piece, "The Four Causes of Health," with its very ancient yet very new idea about health, came spinning into my brain.

I wrote "If Your Heart Condemn You" when I was

moved by a letter a woman wrote to Silent Unity asking us to pray with her; when she was a teen-ager she had committed a sin—she did not say what it had been—and now at eighty-five she was still whipping herself with it.

"Hymn for a Sunrise Service" came to me at a meeting of Unity ministers at Unity Village. They asked me to lead them in a prayer service. It was to be held in the chapel, but it was such a beautiful morning that someone suggested we go outdoors. We all stood clustered at one end of the Bridge of Faith. There under the sky, among the roses, the sun blazing down on our faces, a little wind stirring our hair, the spray from the fountains blowing over us, an invocation of the elements—earth, air, water, and fire—began to pour out of me. Later I had only to recall what I had said and set it down.

The idea in "The Seed and the Harvest" came to me out of a speech I was asked to make, praising two dear friends of mine, a married couple, who had served as Unity ministers for twenty-five years. My only thought as I made the speech was to praise my friends. It was only as I reflected on its content afterward that I realized what a new and happy look at an old truism had emerged in it.

A few years ago when my wife and I were in Florida, a friend gave us tickets for an excursion trip on a boat from Miami to Ft. Lauderdale. Everyone on the boat was a senior citizen, and as the boat moved slowly along, they began singing the song, "It's Later Than You Think." As I sat there, I found myself thinking angrily, "It's absurd for all these old people to be singing this miserable song. There's something wrong about this whole attitude."

Suddenly a sentence leapt into my head—as I say in "Today Is Forever, Forever Today," it is one of the most important insights I have ever had: *We have to live today as if we had all forever, and live forever as if all we had was today.*

After that, writing the article was easy, except that a good ending did not come. So I prayed for one, and the little monk who ends the piece came knocking at my mind in answer to my prayer.

One day as I was thinking about all the people who write to Silent Unity, and their tremendous needs, I said, "God, surely there is something I can say that will be helpful to some of these people." What came to me to say was the simple but true idea that "You Are Not Alone."

I don't recall how all the pieces in the book came to me, but I always write in the hope that I will write something that someone who reads it will need to read.

I believe that what I am saying in most of my writing in this book, and probably in all my books, is that you and I are on an adventure that has a meaning beyond all my power or yours to understand or express—though we must try to understand and express it. We are in a world not mean and humdrum whatever it may sometimes seem, but a world of wonder and perfection beyond our highest vision of perfection— though sometimes we catch glimpses. We are growing toward a destiny beyond our furthest imagining— though in our secret hearts we have always known what we are meant to be.

Of Time and Eternity

When the West thinks of time, it thinks of a river.

When the East thinks of time, it thinks of a still pool. Into the pool a pebble is dropped. A ripple moves from the center to the edge of the pool and then returns on itself again.

Perhaps there is something of both notions in the truth about time. Perhaps time is like a wheel: the wheel goes around and returns on itself, but never in the same place; it has moved on.

Time is like a spiral staircase. At every step there is a narrow aperture through which we can peer as we mount. Each aperture affords a different view. But when we reach the top of the tower, we see all the views at once. Time is a way of looking at eternity. Time is our view of eternity one moment at a time.

Is eternity just a very long time—the past stretched back, the future stretched forward as far as they will go—an infinite number of instants stacked one upon another? At first thought, this is what eternity seems to be.

But when we stretch time back as far as we can and forward as far as we can, and then beyond that and beyond that again, we have only time and yet more time. As far as we can go, beyond us there is only time. When we think in terms of time, we cannot conceive of eternity, we can only conceive of time.

It is somewhat like our thoughts about the Earth. For centuries we thought the Earth was flat, and still as long as we look at the Earth from the standpoint of the Earth, it looks flat. Yet by looking away from it at the stars, we came to see that the Earth is not flat but a globe, a star like other stars. This is the way we must think if we want to think from the outlook of eternity.

Now we read as in a book, syllable by syllable, word by word, page by page. But the book is not a piecemeal work, it is entire, and we can strike through to the gist of it, see it not as a stream of words but for what it means, have it—sense and essence—not by sight but by insight.

A house may be built out of bricks, but a house is more than bricks laid one on another. Eternity is more than the bricks of time, and we must see that it is the house of God and the dwelling place for the human spirit before we can enter in and possess its many mansions.

Now we see as in a mirror darkly, but we can see face to face. Now we see moment by moment, but we can see from the outlook of eternity. This is what in Unity we call seeing the Truth.

Looking in the mirror darkly, we may see imperfection. But the imperfection is not the eternal Truth. It is as though we looked at the stars mirrored in a lake. A wind may ruffle the surface of the lake and distort the stars in the water or even cause them to disappear. But the stars in the heavens are not changed.

In the imperfect mirror of our imperfect knowledge we see an imperfect reflection. But that does not change the one who gazes. We are the ones who gaze.

Could we see things whole, we would see that all things possess wholeness. Things are not less but more than our senses tell us. No description, no matter how accurate, fits anything completely. No name, no matter how apt, is the absolute name.

It is as when we work a jigsaw puzzle. We find a few pieces that fit together and, pondering these, may exclaim, "Clouds!" But when we find a few more pieces, we may decide that what we thought were clouds seem to be birds. And having fitted together still more pieces, we may decide that what we thought were birds look more like flame.

And when at last our minds have found all the pieces of reality and fitted them together, we shall find that what we have is neither cloud nor bird nor flame—but God!

It is not that eternity is more real than time. The One is not more real than the many. As the rainbow is the white light seen through a prism, so time is eternity seen through the prism of the present moment.

There is a sense in which there is no present time. There is also a sense in which there is no time but the present.

The present is the invisible point between the past and the future. It begins to pass away before it has come into existence; that which less than a moment ago was future has now already receded into the past. In this sense, in time there are only past and future. The present is merely the hinge on which they turn. The present is like a page in a book—but one side of the page is past and the other side is future.

Yet in another sense, this nothing, the now, is all the time there is. The future exists only in imagination; the past exists only in memory. Tomorrow is always a look ahead, yesterday a glance back. Both are mere thoughts—memories and hopes. Only the present moment is real.

Listen! At the heart of all that is, the eternal pulse beats, now!

Now is all the time we have, all the time we ever have had, all the time we ever shall have. There has never been, there will never be anything that exists anywhere except in the nothingness of now.

Can this be because now is the point where time and eternity touch? All we can ever have of time is now. But if we lay hold of this never-ceasing, everlasting now, do we not also grasp eternity?

So long as we think of eternity in terms of time—that is, as something going back into the past and forward into the future—we cannot grasp it.

It is like trying to grasp a poem in terms of the letters of the alphabet or a painting in terms of the pigments on the artist's palette. We do not have the house of God; we have only the bricks of time. But by living in the living now, we live in eternity.

It is like four men watching a speeding train.

"Here it comes!" says the first.

"Here it is!" says the second.

"There it goes!" says the third.

But the fourth man is on the train. He neither approaches out of the future nor recedes into the past. He is always in the moving now, and it carries him whither he would go.

Sometimes by the roadside we see a sign: "Where Will You Spend Eternity?" The sign should read: "Where Are You Now?" Eternity is not a future state. God does not ask us to forgo good now to get into His eternal kingdom hereafter. His eternal kingdom is now!

Those who live in the past or future live in a world of ghosts and shadows, of never-was and never-will-be. If now we are not living to the full, we probably did not live to the full before now. The golden age is more than likely a gilded memory. And although it is right to imagine good things happening, we cannot wait until they do, or we will be always waiting, never living.

When you know that right now you have forever, you do not worry over the past or the future. You do not need to loiter; you do not have to hurry. Now you have time for everything—because you have all the time there is, you have the only time there is. Right now!

Do you have one room? Live in it as richly as if it were a hundred rooms. Do you have a hundred rooms?

Live in them as intensely as if they were one room.

Are you the newest apprentice? Is this your first day at work? Work as if it were your last. Is this your last day of work? Tomorrow do you retire? Work as if it were your first.

This is the true art of living: To live each moment to the full, yet know that you have forever.

Each moment is a new and different experience. If it is a moment of gratification, be grateful. If it is a moment of challenge, meet it. It is good to meet what is to be met and to enjoy what is to be enjoyed.

Suppose it is a hard experience; some moments bring bitterly hard things to meet. What then do we do?

We do the only thing we can do—that is, we do what we have to do now. We give what we have to give. We pour out the power we have—the courage, faith, love, wisdom, strength, peace of spirit, and joy of heart.

And perhaps the moment of greatest need may turn out to be the moment of greatest fulfillment. It is when much is asked that much is given. It is when we sink deep that we can rise high. When we come to the end of our own powers, we may find the beginning of God's power.

As the least likely tree may bear the finest fruit, so the least likely experience may be the one from which we gain the most. *The stone which the builders rejected is become the head of the corner.*

The bravest man may cry—as the bravest man did— *My Father, if it be possible, let this cup pass away from me....* But sometimes we find that the draught we sought to put aside is what was needed for our strength. It was not crucifixion. It was resurrection.

To live to the full is to be to the full what we were made to be. We cannot live to the full by being less. And how much we are meant to be! It is no easy or little thing to be a human being!

There is this about time from which we can take heart: Nothing begins except out of endings; nothing ends except by beginning. Time always has two sides. Like a door it cannot close behind us without opening before us. Time is like the pendulum by which we keep it. It is like the sun on which we base it. Has it disappeared in the west? It will reappear in the east.

Time brings us, mainly, little things. This is true for poets, kings, mechanics, and housewives. The biographies of the great record at most a handful of triumphs in a lifetime. But all of us live twenty-four hours a day.

In this we are equal: we all have exactly the same amount of time each day. Awaking at dawn, neither saint nor president has more time than you.

Life does not ask of you, What great things have you done in the past? but only, What are you doing now? What use are you making of the moment that life is now giving you?

Thought by thought, word by word, deed by deed, a life is lived. Only he who finds joy in the passing moment will find contentment in eternity. For the passing moment is eternity. Do not ask if it has much

17

or little. It has all there is. The moment gives of itself to the full. It cannot hold back; it spends itself instantly and completely. Do you give of yourself to the full?

This is the way God gives. He does not make today less perfect because He has tomorrow to make. We have only to look about us, only to raise our eyes—or turn them inward—to see how God gives. Is it a gray day or a sunny one? It makes no difference. God has packed it with extraordinary items and incidents so numerous and various that it is beyond our power to catalog them.

At any moment a single bare room contains such wonder and beauty that our minds would stagger to take a fraction of it in. Consider, for instance, how the room is ringing with music that we do not hear—unless we tune it in!

The room is ringing with a music that we do not hear. It is glowing with a radiance that we do not see. It is fragrant with perfumes that we have no sense of. The room is full of beauty, but it is all the time as if it were in another room. Yet the only wall is in our minds. A thought will topple it.

Now we live by moonlight, but we can live in the sun.
We are never farther from Truth than a thought.
We are never farther from love than a heartbeat.
We are never farther from God than a prayer.
We are never farther from eternity than a moment.
The eternal moment is now.
Live in the *now*.

Live Young!

Ah, to be young forever! How people have longed for that.

The fountain of youth! The elixir of life! The philosopher's stone!

Surely somewhere—in the guarded fruit of a forbidden tree, the enchanted waters of a lost well, a secret formula, an occult incantation, the touch of a sorcerer's wand, the creams and potions from a beautician's vat—there is something to free us from the tyranny of time and keep us young forever!

It is an ancient dream.

Today we are voyaging in space. One of the dreams of the space age is that as we move at rocket speeds, time will but slowly gain upon us. We may be able to move through time as through space, even go backward and become children again.

Time! One of the dimensions in which we live! It winds forward and backward from the present like a scroll, but as it is unrolled before us it is rewound behind us, so that no more than one line is ever visible.

Space seems like a room where we can look around us. But time is like an aperture through which we peer at a peep show.

Today scientists write about space-time and speak of time as if it were the fourth dimension. Time is not the fourth dimension. Time is the cross section of the fourth dimension. It is the only way we three-dimensional creatures can experience the fourth dimension.

Eternity is the fourth dimension. Time and eternity are related as a point is related to a plane or a plane to a cube, if you can remember your geometry. Time is a plane of the cube of eternity. We can see time, but we cannot see eternity.

Now we read the scroll a line at a time. But the scroll is not a line at a time. It is entire—to be grasped at a glance, had we the vision!

To rise beyond the plane of consciousness in which we are caught and see eternity whole—surely this is the true meaning of immortality. This is the nirvana of Buddhists, the samadhi of Hindus, the heaven of Christians.

I am Alpha and Omega, the beginning and the ending, saith the Lord, which is, and which was, and which is to come, the Almighty.

Before Abraham was, I am, said Jesus.

He said also, *Except ye turn, and become as little children, ye shall in no wise enter into the kingdom of heaven.*

Surely, He was telling us that in order to be immortal, we must be immortally young. We must have the spirit and the mind of youth.

What is youth?

Part of being young, certainly, is to believe in immortality. No one ever altogether believes he can cease to exist; but when we are young, we are certain that we have forever. Time is no concern; we have our pockets full of it. We spend it like a prodigal or give it away. The hours stretch out before us endlessly. We may fill them furiously with hubbub or the hardest work, or we may spend a summer lounging under a tree but living in the clouds.

When we are young, the most earthbound of us spends part of his time in the clouds. For youth is imagination, a time of quests and questionings, a time when people dream higher than they ever will again. The young are all poets, though they may never scribble a line. Their thoughts are poetry, for they think in dreams. The logic of dreams is not of the mind but the heart. So the young confound their elders, who want them to be reasonable. But because they are not lost in old facts, they sometimes find new truths.

The young are always venturing beyond the ends of the Earth—and not falling off. And only those who dare the deep can scale the height. The young may fall off cliffs, but also they scale mountains. They may occasionally have wrecks, but also they set new records.

The generations do outstrip one another.

Would you be young?

What are you doing to outstrip yourself and your contemporaries?

Youth is faith. You cannot be bound by facts and be young. Facts are the fences beyond which knowledge has not yet extended. Someone young is always pushing through the fence and enlarging the clearing.

The young annoy their elders by paying no attention to the "Keep Off the Impossible" signs with which age has littered the place. It could only be a man young and free enough to walk on air who would dare to walk on water.

The young have faith in the God within. They feel Him stirring. He is imprisoned, but He will stand free.

The young are rebels, divine rebels, indignant at the iniquities and inequities of the world, refusing to submit to the ukases and usages of age.

The young are incomplete, but they have the passion for perfection. This is the keenness of youth. They are the bow of longing fitted with the arrows of desire, bent to the full by the Archer of Life. Youth is a zest for the best.

To the young, forever is a moment and a moment is forever, and they give themselves to living it.

Youth is not a time of life but a time of being alive. When we are young, we never walk if we can run, and we can dance all night—and do, in our thoughts at least. Oh, the dancing thoughts of youth, playing leapfrog with the ways of the fathers, turning cartwheels through ancient complacencies!

To be young is to be full of vigor. This is what we really want when we say we want to be young again. We want to live at full vigor.

Vigor has little to do with age, as youth has little to do with years. Vigor is possible at any age. Some men and women have more vigor at sixty than at twenty and can still outwork, outwalk, outdream, and out-think most striplings.

Vigor and youth are not gifts vouchsafed us at any age. We win them by being vigorous and youthful. Some are never vigorously young. Some are youthfully vigorous always.

In this world where scientists tell us there are no absolutes, is anything more relative than age?

How old was Albert Einstein at seventy? How old was Thomas Edison at eighty? How old was Charles Fillmore at ninety? How old was Pablo Picasso? How old was Robert Frost?

Not long ago a lass of eighty-eight wrote to me, "I am looking forward to old age."

A rose-cheeked, straight-limbed lad of ninety-five laughed when his children introduced us and said, "Don't believe them. They are lying to you. I am not their father. I am their brother."

Time cannot wither a vital spirit. Age cannot dry up the spring of mind. It is only when we lose faith in our power to grow and settle comfortably down that we begin to be old.

Age complains of youth, "Will it never settle down?" But youth knows that life cannot settle down. Life is a sea voyage. On a sea voyage, to settle down is to sink.

The young do not know what lies ahead. Their powers are untried. They have not found themselves and their meaning.

But which of us has found himself and his meaning?

You may have made some island port of common-sensible contentment, but is this the port you started for? Is this all you hoped to become? Can you remember the dreams of your youth?

The young know that they have not arrived. But no one has arrived. There is not one area of life where we can say, "All has been done that can be done!" The horizon stretches endlessly in all directions. Youth is the jubilant conviction that yet more is to be found—in you and in the world.

Youth is the power to grow. This is the definition of youth.

Stone lasts for centuries by slowing down its processes of change. Yet even the hardest stone must at last disintegrate in the wild dance of its atoms; its stone-stuff will become the roots and leaves of plants, the bone and blood of beasts.

But life is not like stone.

On a warm summer night corn grows so fast you can hear it grow. On a sunny afternoon, a muddy-colored wriggler crawls out of a pond, fastens itself to a stem of grass, and while we watch emerges from its shriveled skin to soar on wings that were not there an hour before, a green-gold dragonfly.

A living thing is like a piece of music. It is not enough to listen to the opening bars or closing chords. You have to hear it played clear through.

You cannot truly take the picture of a living thing. It changes as the shutter clicks.

Will the caterpillar tell you of the butterfly? Or the bullfrog of the polliwog? And how will you know the man? By the babe, or the boy, or the stripling, or the father of the family, or the graybeard?

To live is to change. Nothing alive stands still. A tree may rest in winter, but only to gather strength to grow again in spring.

Life is like fire.

In the heart of every living cell, there is a fire. In the heart of everyone alive, there is a fire.

Fire is change. It never stays the same two seconds together. It lives only by growing. What it touches, it consumes; but what it consumes, it transforms.

When it touches a dead branch, the branch is consumed and transformed! The dead branch becomes dancing flame.

So it is with life. When life kindles inanimate clay, clay can lie still no longer. It has to move and grow and turn into a trout or a bird or a tree or a bit of moss or a human being. It becomes alive.

We cannot live like stone. We must live like fire that lives by growing.

This is the secret of the never-flagging, everlasting vigor of the sun. The sun turns its very atom-stuff into fire and quickens the world around it into ·life.

O God, I pray You, let me like a living sun catch fire with love and burn with truth, igniting all I ever touch with the same love of truth that I have!

Of all Earth's living things, trees have the longest

span of life. And of all living things, they have the longest span of growth. If they live a thousand years, they grow a thousand years. Trees never cease to grow.

To live is to grow.

If we human beings would lengthen the time of our lives, we must lengthen the time of our growth.

You may think there is a limit to the growth you can make.

This may be true of your body. But you are more mind than body, and you are more spirit than mind. In mind and spirit, who dares set a limit on the growth one may make?

A redwood is tall, taking thousands of years to reach its full height. Are you less than a redwood?

Has God not said He created man in His image? How tall is the image of God?

What dimensions has your mind? What span has your spirit?

Are you grown up in your godlikeness?

Oh, what everlasting livingness lies all about us and within us yet to be attained! We are spiritual striplings.

We are children of God.

Youth is the power to grow.

To grow is to be alive.

Would you be alive?

Then live young!

What Is Man?

In the year 1781 the planet Uranus was discovered. Having discovered it, astronomers, peering with crude instruments across almost two billion miles of space computed the course in the heavens it would have to take. But after watching its movement for many years, they became aware that it was not following this course.

Two young men, a Frenchman named Urbain Leverrier and an English college student named John Couch Adams, neither aware of the work of the other, determined to figure out why. To do this, they did not turn a telescope on the skies. They went to work on the problem in their minds. And there, in their minds, without looking at the sky at all, they found the answer.

The only way to account for the deviation in the orbit of Uranus, they said, was that out beyond Uranus, there must be, undiscovered and unknown, yet another planet. Not only that, but this planet had to be in a certain spot in the heavens!

When the astronomers at the Berlin observatory turned their telescope on that spot, there, almost three billion miles away, too small for naked eye to see, no more than a drop of light in a telescope, right where the two young men had said it had to be, was the planet Neptune.

What are we? What is this mind of ours that through

the power of thought can reach across the blind vasts of space, where eye has not penetrated, and declare what must be there? Or, in our own day, reaches down into the depthless abyss of the infinitesimal and, by manipulating imponderable particles that eye has never seen but mind declares must be there, releases unbelievable energies.

We are ourselves like Uranus. We think we know our nature and what may be expected of us. Then we discover that we do not know ourselves at all; we do not follow the predicted course. Beyond the Uranus of our conscious, sentient, reasoning nature—the "me" that eye can see and ear can hear—lies yet some farther Neptune that we must discover before we can say, "That am I."

What am I?

I am aware of my personal limitations. My inadequacies are plain enough. If I look without, I come quickly to my fingertips, my toenails, my hair. If I look within, I come quickly to the end of my knowledge. Beyond this little island stretch outer space and inner spacelessness.

Yet, fire on the farthest outpost of the patriot's country, and you have fired on him. Where then does one stop? And where does one begin? Joan of Arc, burned at the stake, remained rational and calm, praying to the end.

Is this obvious fellow then—this conscious self I am usually so conscious of—what I really am? Is this my true self? Or is this simply part of me, one aspect of me, as my hand is part of me, or my heart, or the invisible wisdom that takes care of the manufacture of red blood cells in my bone marrow, or that in me which flashes ideas into my conscious mind for it to form into a poem?

The truth is that I am not thought, not body, not passion, not feeling, not appetite, not emotion, not will, not conscious mind, not subconscious mind, not any of these things, nor all of them, but more.

I am not to be explained in psychological, nor economic, nor social, nor political, nor biological, nor religious terms. All of these explain aspects of my nature, but aspects only. Separately and altogether, they are not enough. I am yet more.

How much is a human being?

Mind can hold the heavens, all the galaxies that spangle space with stars, yet not be full. Is light swift? Thought can outstrip it. Who shall measure the height of mind or the depth of heart that can feel clear to the heart of being and know its oneness there with every living thing? And how shall we speak of our spirit save to say that it is one with the Spirit of God? As to our powers, when we consider what human beings have done, is there anything that we dare to put beyond them?

We converse across an ocean; we sit in San Francisco and watch events taking place in New York; we fly faster than sound; we cook without fire and cool without ice; we see through night and fog; we make our houses cool by summer and warm by winter and luminous by night; we probe the atom and put its power to work; we explore universes billions of light years distant; we heal disease; we lengthen life; we drain marshes and push back the sea; we make the desert bloom and the wilderness into a garden; we yoke the tides and waterfalls.

What are we that we should do all this?

What is a Mozart who writes a concerto at age eight? or a Grandma Moses who paints a masterpiece at eighty? or a Goethe who at eighteen or eighty-two produces inspired works?

Do you dare assert, "But I am not such as these"?

No one knows the strength of his body to do and bear, the reach of his mind to imagine and perceive, the capacity of his heart to love, the power of his spirit to change his world.

Is there anyone, even the most self-despising person, who has not sometime thought, "I can't do that"—and in the light of his past performance he could not do it—but then, suddenly he found that he was doing it?

I have seen men and women find healing when there seemed no way for them to be healed, and supply when there seemed no means of supply; and I have seen them bring peace to situations and to hearts where there seemed to be no hope but of war. I have seen them lose their possessions or their dear ones or suffer crippling illness, even blindness, and find that they had the resilience to meet the loss so that it became not the end of life but a new beginning. I have seen them keep on when they had nothing left except the spirit to keep on.

It is not only when I see a Mozart or a Grandma Moses that I sense greatness. I sense it when I look at anyone, even a beggar. For this too is life with all life's potentialities, with thoughts that may rise as high as Truth, longings that may reach as far as God, powers that may extend to the limits of faith. All this is there. I know it, and the better I get to know anyone, the more certainly I know it. Under the husks, there it is.

And everyone knows it too. For a beggar might change places with a king, change his rags for the king's robe, his ignorance for the king's knowledge, his weakness for the king's power, but his self for the king's self? Never. Why not? Because he knows deep down in his inmost reality, in the deep center of his being, in the real self of himself, "I am the very best that is!"

How shall anyone say of himself or another, "This am I, no more"? Did one do a deed? Another shall do as much and more. He who did most of all said, . . . *The works that I do shall he do also; and greater works than these shall he do.* And He said, *If ye have faith . . . nothing shall be impossible unto you.*

One night outside of Houston, Texas, a truck crashed into a tree, pinning the driver, unconscious, in the twisted steel of the capsized cab, which caught fire. Two trucks were hooked to each end of the wreck to try

31

to straighten it out so that the doors could be gotten open and the driver removed. This did not succeed. Men attacked the doors with crowbars, but could not pry them open. Meanwhile, the fire reached the feet of the driver.

Then out of the dark stepped a man. He took hold of the door of the truck, which four trucks and men with crowbars had not been able to open, and he tore it from its hinges. He reached inside, bent back the steering wheel, plucked out of the floor as if they were straws the brake and clutch pedals in which the driver's feet were caught, and with his bare hands beat out the flames.

Still they could not get the driver out. So he wedged himself into the cab and began to straighten up. Those who were there said that they could hear the steel popping as the roof rose, and the man kept pushing up that steel roof till eager hands were able to reach in and remove the driver.

Without a word, the man disappeared then. But they found him a few days later. He was a black man named Charles Dennis Jones. When they asked him how he had been able to do what he had done, he said, simply, "You never know what you can do till you see another man hurting." It is not only Charles Dennis Jones who has power in him to help the hurting. It is every one of us.

The simple words of this man point the way to find this power in ourselves. It is to forget ourselves and think about others. To find ourselves we must lose ourselves. For we come to ourselves only when we go beyond ourselves and give ourselves to something more, to other men and women or to God.

We come to ourselves most often in prayer, for in prayer we go beyond our little self to the great Self-lessness, which is perhaps the best name for our true identity.

Identify yourself with God, as Jesus did. Give your mind to God, your heart, your life to God, and you will find that God gives Himself through you, His mind your mind, His heart your heart, His life your life.

You have powers you never knew you had. You are more than you have thought yourself to be. Believe!

A bird flies into a room. We open all the windows and try to edge it toward one. But often it continues to flutter blindly from corner to corner. Yet the windows are open. Nothing restrains it but itself. The whole sky beckons if it will but fly forth.

So we flutter about the little room in which we find ourselves, come to blind corners in our reasoning, beat vainly against the windowpanes that are our senses. Yet the windows of our faith are open upon infinity itself, if we will but fly forth.

When the littleness in us grows less, the greatness increases. When we are no longer bound to selfish ends, we are free.

When the separateness in us is dissolved, we are at one.

When we let go our limitations, we find ourselves beyond them.

Beyond them is God.

As beyond a wave there is the sea, and as the wave is not separate from the sea but extends back into the sea and shares the sea's strength, so beyond body, beyond mind, there is the selfless self where each one of us knows that he is not separate and little and powerless but one with the Good Omnipotent itself. It is here that each of us knows, "I am the very best that is!"

Your Unknown World

We live in a time of reaching out. We send rockets into space to probe the moon, Venus, Mars, the immensity beyond. We train giant telescopes on worlds so distant that measurement seems meaningless. We bring together our most brilliant minds, erect complex, ingenious machines, spend billions of dollars—even to begin the conquest.

What is out there? we ask, and dream what it will be like to journey into emptiness.

This is a noble project—to explore the world around us. Our minds shake the tree of the world, and the fruit of the knowledge of things has come dropping into our hands.

We are all dwellers in space; we make our habitation among stars and molecules. Out of their stuff we build our homes and even the bodies with which we build.

Our very word "real" comes from the ancient Latin word that means "a thing." So much are we a part of the world.

Yet, real as the world of things may seem, what person thinks of himself as a "thing"? There are times when we all feel more like observers of the world than a part of it. We view it, as it were, from somewhere else.

The outer world is all around us. We seem to live and move and have our being in it. It washes over us like a sea. Yet we sense that we ourselves are not of this sea but only voyagers through its deeps.

We are not children of the world but only dwellers in it. We are children of God.

If there is an outer world in which we dwell, there is also an inner world, at least as real, as vast in extent, as strange and rich and varied. It is not a world of space and time, of things and dimensions. It is a world of thought and feeling, of mind and spirit.

Here are deeps at least as deep as a sea. Here are heights at least as high as a mountain. Here are valleys; here are rivers; here are storms and calms, green pastures and still waters, dark nights and rosy dawns. We have in us a world.

And today, if we ask, "What is out there?" We have begun to ask, "What is in there?"

We have become aware that there is an unknown world within us.

It is a world about which we know very little. We are about to explore the moon—and most of us have never explored ourselves.

We are full of desires, thoughts, feelings, powers, and potentialities that we are almost unaware of. Sometimes we seem to live like a water skipper on the surface of a deep well. But we are not merely a skipper on the surface; we are the well and all that it contains, its creatures and its deeps, at the source one with all the waters of the world.

Have you ever thought how little you know about you?

What is the world within you like? Where is it? When you turn within, where do you turn? Is it to some center in your body? or in your head?

Has it ever occurred to you that your inner world is not a place? It is not inside your body or your head. Your inner world is not "a-whereness"; it is awareness.

Pick up a book, observe its covers, turn its pages, note the black lines of type on the white sheets of paper. Is this the book?

It is the outward form of the book, but there is infinitely more to a book than this. A book exists more in the inner world than in the outer world. A book is not so much an object in space as it is an idea in mind. Every copy of it can be burned, yet that book will remain as alive as ever—as long as we hold it in mind.

If this is true of a book, is it not much more true of a human being? His physical appearance is among the least important things about him—and becomes even less important the better we get to know him. After a time we may scarcely be aware of it; people who are close to us change appearance, and we do not even see the change.

It is what you are within that is important. People, like books, may sometimes have lovely covers and yet have little substance inside. And great books and people often come to our hand dog-eared, plain, and worn. But the truth and the beauty shine from within.

So it is with you.

Within you are your true treasures—treasures yet

untouched. Here are mines of mind richer than Golconda, resources of spirit beside which the wealth of the Indies is paltry. The discoveries that we have made, the powers that we have tapped—these are small beside the powers within that lie waiting to be tapped, the discoveries within that lie waiting to be made.

In us, for instance, is a power to heal. It is at work all the time. Most of the time we are unaware of it; it is quietly repairing cells, carrying off wastes, nourishing tissues, and healing wounds. But occasionally it reveals itself in one of us in some remarkable way. A man is mortally ill; and suddenly, with no explanation, the growth vanishes, the wound heals, the heart restores itself. If there has been prayer—if, say, the man has gone to Lourdes or written to Silent Unity—we exclaim, "A miracle!" If not, we just wonder and rejoice.

But the fact is that this inner power of healing, of life, is not an extraordinary power. It is in all of us all the time. It is a natural part of our inner world. But we have not yet learned how to make it work through us.

Constantly, twenty-four hours a day, part of us is supervising all the fantastically complicated operations of our bodies. Effortlessly, in a single cell, the super-scientist in us performs functions that the world's most learned chemists cannot duplicate in acres of factories.

And these are only a fraction of the powers the mind-giant in us possesses.

There are people who in a moment do mathematical feats of unbelievable difficulty. Almost as fast as anyone can present a problem, they give the answer.

There are others who have equally remarkable powers of memory. They have only to glance at a page once to have it fixed in mind for years.

In our time we are beginning to explore yet other powers. Experimenters in the field of parapsychology are discovering that we have powers we have not even dreamed of.

Space does not exist in the world within us; we are anywhere with the speed of thought. Time does not exist; we are in the past or future as easily as in the present. Now we go only in imagination—but the power is there—and we shall learn to use it, not merely to imagine but actually to experience.

Is there one of us who does not have a sense of a world within at least as vast and strange as the world outside? Is there one of us who has not now and then touched powers beyond his common ones?

Sometimes we catch only a momentary flash of something not quite understood. But sometimes we see something happen that makes us suddenly aware that there is a power within beside which the power in the atom, the power that holds the stars in their courses, is puny.

A Moses needs to part a Red Sea. The Mormons need to stem an invasion of crickets. A George Müller needs to feed the hungry boys in his orphanage at Bristol,

England. An Eddie Rickenbacker needs to feed the men afloat with him in a rubber life raft.

Our greatest triumphs are all triumphs of mind. Someone lays hold on an idea in mind and finds—oh, ever-recurring miracle!—that he has grasped the world of things outside him and changed it nearer to his heart's desire.

A man named Henry Ford was born more than a hundred years ago, the son of a farmer. He changed the habits of his nation. What with? With the intuitive power within him.

A man named Mohammed, an illiterate caravan guide, changed a few tribes of desert nomads into a force that conquered much of the Earth, founded a great culture, and established a religion that is still influencing more than four hundred million people. Where did he find such a capacity? One night in a cave, communing alone, he had a revelation from within.

A fourteen-year old girl named Joan, the illiterate daughter of a poor peasant in a remote part of France, heard voices telling her to go to her king and lead his army to free her country from the enemies that had seized most of it. She did it! Where did she hear the voices? Within.

A man named Shakespeare, with only a grammar-school education, wrote the most beautiful English and the greatest plays ever written. Where did the words come from? From within him.

A man named Mozart began to compose music when

he was five years old, and he wrote so many unsurpassed pieces that it takes a catalog just to list the titles. Where did this music flow from? From within.

A man named Edison, deaf and with only three months in public school, was responsible for so many inventions that our whole way of life has been changed by them—I write this sentence by the light of one. What did he draw on? The world within him.

A man named Jesus, a carpenter's son, living in an obscure village in an obscure province that He never left, changed everyone of us. Where did the power come from to bring about this change? He told us. *The Father who dwelleth in me, he doeth the works,* He said. And He said further to each one of us, "God is within you."

These are geniuses, prophets, saviours, we say. But the greatest of them promised that we could do even greater things than He did.

These men and women did not touch a power that only they had. They touched a power that all of us have.

In us is a creative spirit. We touch it occasionally, and out of the unknown, like sparks from a cosmic fire, come revelations of truth, visions of beauty, fresh forms of life and joy. Not out of a cloud nor out of the hand of a Zeus the lightning flashes, but out of ourselves. In us are the everlasting springs of life. In us is the secret place of the Most High.

Remember the story of the king's son who was taken

from his father at birth and brought up in a wood-chopper's hut, believing he was a woodchopper.

Why are we living like woodchoppers? We are—all of us—a king's sons and daughters.

What are we doing in this hut of husks? We are the children of Mind, made in the image of a divine idea. We have a kingdom that is ours for the claiming—the kingdom of consciousness, the inner country of the heart and mind, the world of ideas.

Is there a chart that we can follow as we make this unknown world our own? Is there a map of mind, an atlas of the heart?

Some who have gone before us have left records of their explorations. Cartographers of spirit, they tell us how we may begin our voyage.

"Be still, and know," they say and lay down disciplines of thought and feeling and desire.

Enter into thy closet, and when thou hast shut thy door, pray to thy Father which is in secret. This the Way-Shower told us. *Follow me,* He said. *Seek, and ye shall find.*

But we have scarcely made a landing on this shore. Before us lies a hemisphere of being.

Is there infinity outside? Do not think that there is less than infinity inside. In is just like out—it is without boundaries. You have a world within you infinite in extent and in potentiality, an unknown world where you must make the quest and conquest of yourself.

How high can you go? As high as you can hope.

How deep can you go? As deep as you can feel.

How far can you go? As far as you can imagine.

Go as far as thought will take you, and when you have come to the perfection of truth, you will have found beauty of spirit.

Go as far as spirit will take you, and when you have come to the perfection of beauty, you will have found a heart of love.

Go as far as love will take you, and when you have come to the perfection of love, you will have found the fulfillment of desire.

The fulfillment of desire is God.

The One We All Might Be

There was One who showed us what we all might be. He did not so much tell us what our lives should be like, He lived the life that we might live.

The One we all might be had faith in other people. He saw in them potentialities that others overlooked. He knew them to be capable of more than they themselves thought. He inspired sinners to become saints, social outcasts to become public benefactors, weaklings to become towers of strength. He changed common fishermen into "fishers of men."

The One we all might be saw through life's imperfections—through sickness and doubt, through poverty and fear, through hatred and pride, even through death—and He called forth wholeness, faith, joy, love, and life. He showed us what life might be—lived to the utmost of its possibilities. He showed us what a person might be who held to the highest and best in himself.

How hard we find it to love one or two persons! Yet He showed us that it is possible to learn to love all. How many hours we have wasted in resentment! Yet this One showed us that it is possible to live free from hate.

He knew how much a loving heart is worth, He had a sense of right values. He was able to judge not by appearances; able to put first things first; able to see how much more important than material treasures are the treasures of heart and mind.

He saw people as they are, flesh-and-blood creatures with physical needs and desires. Not once did He suggest, "It will be better for your soul if your body suffers, so I will not help you." Those who were sick, He healed; those who were hungry, He fed. He knew that love does not exact pain-payments as the price of spiritual growth.

This is no man of sorrows, though He wept. Though He suffered, His was no tragic life. Even His death was not truly tragic, for how quickly the darkness of Calvary was wiped away in the light of Easter morning! The energy released by the overcoming that He made at death is still flooding, two thousand years later, into millions of lives.

His was no easy life, but surely people are not given their tremendous mental and spiritual powers in order to have a problem-free existence.

This One had human needs and human problems. Had He not been endowed with human nature, then He could not have meant to us what He means. We could not aspire to put on His character. We could not hope to imitate His life. Though this be "very God of very God," this is also "very man of very man."

How human was His love for His family! Almost His last act, as He hung on the Cross, was to commit His mother to the care of His best friend.

He was weary and He rested by the well. He was thirsty and He said, *Give me to drink.* He was angered at people's inability to see the truth—though never at the people themselves—and He expressed His anger in flaming words and sometimes in hot deeds. When He saw the sadness of His friends, He wept. He shrank from pain as all people do. He cried, *Remove this cup from me,* though He added, *Nevertheless not my will, but thine, be done.*

He had moments of doubt and cried out like a child, *My God, my God, why hast thou forsaken me?*

Yet, He was intimately aware of His oneness with God. He was human, but always He saw Himself as more than a human being; He saw Himself as a spiritual being with spiritual powers.

He fed people with bread when they needed it; He healed their bodies and minds. But He knew also that we cannot live by bread alone, we must have the living bread of inspiration, and this He offered never-ceasingly.

He saw life clear and saw it whole, and He saw Himself as part of the whole, just as He knew that the whole was part of Him. He saw that in the truest sense He and the whole were one. He could say to those who would see God, *Look on me.*

Here was no splinter of a man, lonely or afraid, wondering as to His meaning and function in the vastness of the universe. This One knew that all of us are one with one another and with the whole.

47

He knew the truth about Himself, not in abstract words but in every fiber of His being. He was so conscious of His godlikeness that He was never anything less.

He was aware of His spiritual power. He called forth no armies of angels, caused no signs to be displayed in the heavens, but always He was the master of Himself and of powers beyond Himself.

This One was able to focus all the energies that we dissipate on trivialities, fears, and hatred on whatever problem was presented to Him; and before the fierce heat of His spiritual power the problem was melted away.

Was there a multitude to be fed? With what was at hand the need was met.

Was there one who was dumb or blind, one who was lame or mad? *The blind receive their sight, and the lame walk, the lepers are cleansed, and the deaf hear, the dead are raised up....*

Even over death He had power, for He knew that in truth death has no power or reality. Though He died, it was only to rise again.

So great was the power this One laid hold of that whatever He was called on to meet, whether for Himself or another, He met victoriously.

Yet even in His use of power He taught us much. Though this One was the most powerful one who ever lived, He was also the most responsible. There is no instance when He used His power to force another to do

His will. This was no Zeus hurling thunderbolts at His enemies. When the people of His hometown tried to mob Him, He did not call down angels to defend Him; He slipped quietly away.

The One we all might be showed us how humble true greatness is!

He could be humble because He understood His worth. *Who say ye that I am?* He asked His apostles, and Peter's answer rings across a score of centuries, *Thou art the Christ, the Son of the living God.* Knowing who He was, He did not have to puff Himself up with titles and pretense. He could wash the feet of His friends. He could mix with the lowliest and the least worthy, with no awareness of their lowliness or their unworthiness. *Neither do I condemn thee,* He said.

Yet He had an unfailing sense of His own worth. He let His feet be bathed in precious ointments. Even when He appeared as a criminal on trial for His life, He had such poise that He unnerved the Roman dignitary, Pilate.

He was meek, not weak. He avoided quarrels when He could; but when He had to engage in argument, His wit shone like a sword. His was the meekness that springs from the awareness of strength; His was the humility that springs from the awareness of worth.

He was filled with spiritual light, but He had great practical wisdom, too. He had an infinite understanding of people and of the springs of action in them. He saw the causes of unhappiness, and He knew the way to happiness. He knew that *every idle word that men shall speak, they shall give account thereof.* He knew that it is not enough for people to control their actions, they must control their thinking, too. He believed in obeying laws, but He repeatedly reminded His friends that laws were made for men, and not men for laws.

He was as much a man of action as He was a man of faith and love. Though He was always in close communion with His Father, though He spent days and nights and even weeks in prayer and meditation, He knew that heaven had to be established not only in mind and heart but also had to be made a living reality in the physical universe.

He did not withdraw from the world, nor did He allow His apostles to withdraw. He sent them out, not to meditate but to *preach the gospel to the poor . . . to heal the brokenhearted, to preach deliverance to the captives, and recovering of sight to the blind, to set at liberty them that are bruised.*

He was without fear for personal safety, without worry about personal needs, for He knew that all the powers of the universe work together for those who are in harmony with them. Life clothed the lilies of the field and cared for the sparrows—why should He fear? He was not concerned as to whether what He did was financially profitable, only as to whether it was profitable to mankind. He was concerned only with the truth.

He did not lack for shelter, though He had *nowhere*

to lay his head. He could say to the storm, *Peace! Be still!* The waves could not sweep away His clear, sure calm. Serene in His purpose, He never lost His sense of direction.

This One embodied what we only envision. But however nobler than our own His character may be, however superior to our own His powers may seem, however larger than our own His accomplishments may loom, this is what we all might be. His is the life we all might live.

Certainly this One believed this to be true.

Follow me, He said. *He that believeth on me, the works that I do shall he do also; and greater works than these shall he do.* He that believes! *All things are possible to him that believeth.*

This is God in incarnation, as we are God in aspiration. When Principle incarnates in human form, this is the kind of life that results. But Principle is incarnate in all of us. This is the life toward which all of us are moving. It is our own faces that look down at us from Calvary, and it is in our own flesh that we feel the stir of Easter morning. He knew this, and He said, *I in them, and thou in me, that they may be made perfect in one.*

What height of fulfillment, what depth of compassion, what breadth of understanding might be ours—if we were all that we might be!

Ours to love with a love that excludes none but gives itself to all.

To have a sense of right values, placing spiritual things first, yet using spiritual powers to transform the physical world.

To be master of self and superior to circumstance.

To be humble of spirit, yet conscious of eternal worth.

To be at peace, yet to be a center of energy.

To be God-centered, a focus through which His power flows freely in joyous achievement.

To be unlimited in vision and to attain what we envision.

To experience the fullness of compassion, yet to live to the fullness of joy.

To be able to help all who turn to us, to bless the lives we touch, to turn sorrow into joy, hate into love, sickness into health, lack into fulfillment, death into life.

To be one with the essential harmony at the center of things.

To be free from worry and fear about our physical necessities in the faith that this is a hospitable universe.

To see ourselves in relation to the whole, merging the fraction of self in the integer of God!

This is what we all might be.

The Victorious Spirit

There are times in the life of everyone when he comes to a place where he feels that he cannot go on. Especially at a time like this, when great demands are made on all of us, many people find themselves faced with problems that seem beyond their powers to cope with. Adjustments are not easy to make. But they can be made.

It is often just when we have struggled until we feel that we cannot go on that the pattern of victory begins to appear, and suddenly we see that our struggles have not been wasted, that a work has been done that was no less effective because it was invisible.

Sometimes when a person has striven to the utmost limit of his capacity and can see no progress, an insidious something inside of him may whisper that it is foolish to continue the struggle. Yet there are tremendous resources still left in him, hidden, undeveloped resources of courage, faith, love, mastery, and perseverance; and if he makes the effort he will call them forth.

In his great book "Wind, Sand, and Stars" Antoine de Saint Exupéry tells the story of Guillaumet, an aviator whose plane crashed in a storm in the Andes.

Guillaumet had been stumbling through a trackless waste of peaks and ice for three days and nights during which he had been unable to rest even for a minute because of the freezing cold. At last he felt that he could go no farther, and he lay down in the snow. Instantly the numbness brought on by cold began stealing through him. It felt pleasant and peaceful. But fifty feet ahead he saw a rock, and he thought: If I lie here my body will never be found, because it will be carried down into the ravine when the snow melts in the spring; but if I can get to that rock I can prop myself behind it, and then my body will be found and my wife will be able to collect the insurance, which she will need very much.

He staggered to his feet and started toward the rock and he kept going until the rescue party found him three days later.

A friend of mine who had to find his way out of a serious psychoneurotic state told me: "The hardest thing was to make an effort. Until you have been down where I was you cannot imagine how much effort it takes merely to eat. The act of choosing a shirt, lacing a shoe, or tying a necktie became an almost insuperable task. I wanted to curl up in bed and lie there." But he did not lie there. He did not withdraw from life or let life withdraw from him. He got up and fought the battle of himself and won it.

Life demands of us effort, but life is worth the effort. We would not want an effortless life. Circumstances may buffet us and even knock us down, and sometimes we may not seem to have the strength to rise again; but if we persevere we find that we can get up and go on. When we refuse to give way to thoughts of inadequacy and fear or feelings of frustration and bitterness, and employ our physical, mental, and spiritual energies in constructive endeavors, we find that we have undreamed-of capacities. Life can be lived victoriously and abundantly.

It is not conditions and circumstances that determine the measure of our achievement and satisfaction. The exploits of people with handicaps, of the maimed, the blind, the deaf, and the psychoneurotic fill many books. Toscanini was so nearsighted that he could not see the score when conducting; Byron had a club foot; Homer and Milton were blind; Sir Walter Scott was a bedridden invalid; Beethoven was deaf; Dostoevski and de Maupassant were epileptic; Franklin D. Roosevelt did not have full use of his legs.

As a matter of fact, who does not have some kind of handicap, whether it be physical, mental, emotional, educational, social, or economic? But a handicap is not always a handicap; it may become an extra incentive. Often in order to overcome a handicap a person has to put forth such prodigious effort that sources of power are stirred up in him that enable him not only to overcome the handicap but to achieve a life of previously unimagined satisfaction.

A thousand centuries ago the Spirit of God in him led the human being out of his cave and set before him a dream and a hope. It led him along the perilous way where not even the mastodon and the saber-toothed tiger, for all their marvelous physical development, could survive; but Spirit within him enabled him to survive and even to grow.

That Spirit is your heritage. It will help you now in the arduous adventure that is life. We do not mean that it will make your problems smaller. But the Spirit of God in you will make you bigger. It may not preserve you from reverses, but it will bring you through defeat undefeated; and it will help you to know that "if hopes were dupes, fears may be liars." It will give you the courage to accept life for what it is, and then it will give you the faith to make something more out of it. There is a spirit in you that is braver than your fears, stronger than your doubts. There is a spirit in you, a victorious spirit, and you can meet whatever comes to pass.

On Armistice Day in 1918, at the end of the first World War, an American sculptor named George Grey Barnard happened to be in Paris. Inspired by the wild jubilation of the crowds, he planned a great monument to peace, a hundred feet high and sixty feet wide, to be called "The Rainbow Arch." He knew that it would take many years and much money to construct it, but he was willing to make any sacrifice. As soon as he could he returned to New York and rented a deserted carbarn for a studio.

He was not a young man when he began this work. His heart was giving him trouble, and the doctors warned him repeatedly that if he did not quit he would

56

drop dead; but he paid no attention to them. His age and physical condition forced him to work more slowly, but he kept doggedly at it. After eighteen years—he was then seventy-three years old—the end of his task was in sight.

Then one morning a policeman came to his home and asked him to come with him. He was driven to the carbarn studio. The policeman led him through the door, and there he saw a sight that could have stopped a younger, stouter heart than his. His long years of toil lay around him in ruins. Vandals had broken in during the night and smashed all his sculptures.

But the heart of this man of seventy-three had a strength that was infinitely beyond anything that the stethoscopes of the doctors had been able to measure. He cleared away the wreckage and began all over again; and when he died, the great figures of his arch were finished, and he left money for the completion of the entire project, which stands today not far from his home in New York.

So when I find myself wanting to give up, I think of that old sculptor in the carbarn, who at seventy-three could take so cruel a blow, and, knowing that eighteen years' work had been wasted, that he was sick, that his faculties were failing, that he had but little time, could start all over again and do what he did.

Truly the Spirit of God in us is a magnificent spirit. When we face the impossible we discover that we face it with capacities greater than we knew; for we do not face it alone; there is a Spirit in us!

If you have ever been on a high mountain peak, you know that far above the timber line where the elements are so fierce that even the rocks are shattered and powdered by their force, vegetation flourishes and flowers bloom in the crevices between the bare rocks. Life is the mightiest force in the world, and the highest expression of life is the living spirit in us human beings. The dauntless, creative, resilient spirit in us is mightier than circumstances.

For while the tired waves, vainly breaking,
*   Seem here no painful inch to gain,*
Far back, through creeks and inlets making,
*   Comes silent, flooding in, the main.*
And not by eastern windows only,
*   When daylight comes, comes in the light;*
In front the sun climbs slow, how slowly!
*   But westward, look, the land is bright!*

You Are the Master

It is easy to be optimistic when everything is going well. But when you are faced with difficult conditions, when you are in pain, or when you have failed or have lost a loved one, it is then that your resources are really put to the test.

Do you have a goal you wish to reach? Do you have a need that is not easy to meet? Do you need health of body? Do you lack peace of mind? Do you seek financial success or artistic achievement? Do you want more love, more friends, more happiness? Do you have to overcome some personal shortcoming?

To satisfy your need or reach your goal you must assert your mastery. You master circumstance or you are mastered by it. You control your moods and emotions or you are controlled by them.

It is, of course, one thing to tell yourself to assert your mastery and another thing to do it. It is easy to shout from the sidelines, "Be brave. Be firm. Press forward." It is another matter when you yourself must press through difficulties toward the goal.

Then you must put forth the highest spiritual effort of which you are capable and continue to do so unceasingly, facing your fears and doubts, going forward in spite of pain, learning to focus all your energy—physical, mental, and spiritual—on the attainment of your goal.

Do not think that you do this by an act of will. No one ever became the master of his life by merely willing to. You must make the decision that you are going to be the master. But this decision is only the first step. Then you must keep on taking steps.

Trying to master yourself and life by an act of will is like trying to pull yourself up a mountain by your thumbs. To assert your mastery you must use all the faculties you have. You must put your whole self—body, mind, and Spirit—to work.

The essential thing is that you assert your mastery in your heart. Any words, statements, thoughts, feelings, actions, or steps that you can take to do this are good.

It helps to use such a statement as *Christ dominion is mine. I am illumined, glorious, splendid, free!* or *All power is given me in mind and body. I am the power and the mastery.*

Do not think of yourself as a slave of circumstance. Do not think of yourself as weak and inadequate, poor and unloved. Do not give power to old habits of thought by dwelling on them and acting as if they were true. If you feel yourself swept by self-pity or self-condemnation, set your mind to evaluating and understanding and appreciating yourself instead.

When old habits of thought try to reassert themselves, face them and think them through. Question them. Challenge them. Refuse to let them take control. Start asserting the reasons why they are not true.

Start finding reasons for your mastery.

Practice prayer. Pray not only at regular intervals, such as immediately after waking and before falling asleep, but whenever doubt or fear about any condition arises.

Turn your mind and energy to constructive tasks. Play the piano. Work at a hobby. Work in the garden. Help somebody in need of help. Keep building new reactions by doing new things. There are a thousand and one things to be done. Find the things you want to do.

The old habits may rise up and rise up again. You must face them and face them again.

Do you want to achieve the mastery? You must determine that you can achieve it. Do not doubt it. Believe that you can. Even if you cannot believe it, assert it. And keep on asserting it.

Keep on! There is the key to achievement. Keep on and keep on keeping on! Find reasons for wanting to keep on. Find reasons for having to keep on.

Everybody has times when he gets discouraged. It is nothing to lose heart—if you keep on. For if you keep on, you will take heart again. It is nothing to be fearful—if you keep on. Your fear can even be a goad to drive you forward.

Sometimes the very desperation of our plight makes us take action. When we find ourselves on the face of a precipice with nothing to do but climb or fall, we will exert energy we never dreamed we had to get to the top. If we have only a gentle slope to climb, we may be content to stop halfway up.

That is probably one of the reasons why prayer sometimes works in urgent cases when it does not seem to work in what are apparently much easier matters. Faced by a desperate need, we pray as we have never prayed before—and our prayer is answered. That is probably the reason why people with great handicaps so often achieve great goals in life.

So it is well to keep in mind when we seem to be having a hard time that there may be help in the very urgency of the need.

Whatever the situation we find ourselves in, the important thing is the attitude that we take toward it.

If we want victory, we must prepare for victory. Victories are not won by planning for defeat. When Cortes landed his handful of Spaniards in Mexico to conquer the powerful and populous Aztec Empire, he burned his ships. He envisioned only victory, and despite hardship, despite setbacks, he won victory.

We can accept failure and find all sorts of excuses for it; or come what may, we can push on, rise up no matter how many times we fall down, and turn even failure into success. Whatever reasons we may find for doubting our ultimate success, we must push forward, for only if we push forward can we even hope to reach our goals.

Everyone who has ever set out to better himself or his life has heard the voice of despair cry, "Turn back, turn back!"

When things are hardest, that is when we must try hardest. If we suffer a setback, that is when we must press ahead.

When we make a good struggle and win through to considerable confidence and strength, perhaps even feeling somewhat proud of our progress, and then some unlooked-for blow falls, crushing us—that is a crucial moment.

In such moments we can give up or get up. We can give in to the old habits of thought and accept defeat. Or we can pull ourselves together, bind up our wounds, dust ourselves off, and keep on! To do that is to assert our mastery.

We are like one who has a mountain to climb. The path is not always an ascending one. Sometimes we may go down into deep valleys. Sometimes we may fight our way through fierce storms. But that is when we must decide who is the master—ourselves or circumstances?

When everything in us cries, "Turn back, turn back!" that is when we must decide whether we or our fears are going to shape our destiny.

Are we going to be driven about by every changing wind of circumstance, turned back by every looming cloud of fear? Or are we going to push forward in spite of difficulty, in spite of fear?

Sooner or later everyone comes to a place where he must take a stand. If we decide that we will rise superior to circumstance, if we take command of ourselves and seize the reins of our own fate, from that moment on we live on a new level.

We may have to struggle to maintain our command. The old ways of thought, the old habits and reactions may seek to reassert themselves. But we will find that our whole attitude toward life is changed. We will have new powers, new energy, new understanding, new love. We will have a sense of purpose in life. Our lives will broaden and deepen. Our whole personality will expand. However hard we may have to struggle against the old ways of thought, we will have a peace of mind and a joy in living beyond anything we ever knew.

You can take your stand now. The infinite potentialities of a child of God open before you. Before you lies fulfillment. Before you lies the joyous awareness of the truth about yourself. You can be free.

Christ in you is the Lord of life. Through Him all power is given you in mind and in body. Take your stand. Make your choice. Assert your mastery as a spiritual being.

You are the master.

The Pollyanna

There are four possible attitudes to take in a situation.

You can believe that things are going to work out and work hard to see that they do.

You can believe that things are going to work out and do nothing about them yourself.

You can believe that things are not going to work out but nevertheless work hard yourself.

You can believe that things are not going to work out and resign yourself to defeat.

It is easy to see that the second and fourth attitudes have little to recommend them.

The one who has the third attitude may succeed in his endeavors, but how he suffers with them. "This is a hard, hard task," he groans under the heavy burden not only of his task but of his thoughts about it.

Surely the first attitude is best of all. The person who has it is most likely to succeed, and what is more, he has a spirit of joy as he works toward success.

Those who think of themselves as deep enough to be discouraged about things say that those who are encouraged about things have a shallow view of life; they call such people pollyannas.

If a pollyanna is someone who refuses to face facts, certainly none of us wants to be one. We cannot get rid of facts by pretending that they are not there. But we can face facts and still know that good is there, whether we can see it at first or not. It has to be there because God is there. And we can seek in every situation to find and bring forth God's good.

A pollyanna is not a person who refuses to face facts. He is a person who refuses to accept them. He does not believe that the passing facts are the ultimate truth. The ultimate truth is always good. This is a good world. It is good because He who made it is good. Because He who made it is good, there must be good in everything. The pollyanna, the positive thinker, the Unity student looks for this good and does all he can to bring it forth.

Jesus refused to be limited by facts. No matter what appearances might be, He looked for the good, expected the good, and did all He could to bring forth the good. Jesus knew that the world is the work of the good God. He was in the Good Presence always. Good was never far from Him.

When He was asked to feed the multitude that had come to hear Him and found out that they had only a few loaves and fishes, He did not say that the facts indicated He would not be able to do it. Beyond the facts He saw the everywhere-at-hand bounty of God, and He called it forth and fed the people.

Even when they told Him that Lazarus was three days dead, He did not submit to the fact of death. Instead He decreed, expecting the good, *Lazarus, come forth.*

Remember how much He approved of the army captain who asked Him to heal his servant. When Jesus offered to go, the captain told Him it would not be necessary. *"Speak the word only, and my servant shall be healed,"* he said. Why did Jesus think so highly of this man? Because here was a man of faith like Himself; here was a man who expected and believed in the possibility of good.

Jesus did not see a hungry multitude; He saw them fed by the infinite bounty. He did not see sick people; He saw them whole, alive with the aliveness of divine life. He did not see drab facts; He saw the radiant truth. *Ye shall know the truth, and the truth shall make you free,* He said. *Be of good cheer.*

Never once did He say to anyone who came to Him for help, "You have to accept the facts." He said over and over in many different words, *Ask and it shall be given unto you; seek, and ye shall find; knock, and it shall be opened unto you.*

I like the story of the little girl who looked up at the church steeple and said, "What's the plus sign doing up there?" It is more than a coincidence that the symbol of Christianity, the cross, is also a plus sign, the sign of the positive, the positive-minded, the positive-hearted.

Usually when people start talking about facing facts, they mean looking at the worst side of them. Facts are many-sided. Is it wrong to look for the best side rather than the worst?

It is said that Thomas Edison made 10,000 experiments that failed before he made an electric bulb that lighted. What a fantastic amount of foolish optimism he must have had! Could someone who thought things were going to turn out badly have kept going? I do not believe it.

Wilhelm Roentgen came to work one morning and found that a photographic plate he had left in a drawer was fogged. He might have bemoaned the fact. Instead, he discovered X rays—and opened the atomic age.

Charles Goodyear dropped some elastic gum he was experimenting with on the stove. The fact certainly is that the gum was spoiled—but the truth is that the rubber industry was founded.

An apple fell and hit Sir Isaac Newton on the head. The fact is that the apple probably raised a lump—but the truth is that it brought forth the theory of gravitation.

In the Nova Scotia mine explosion of 1958, men were entombed for days without light, food, or water. They were keenly aware of their plight, but when one of them became depressed, the others crept around him and said all the things they could think of to encourage him. They would not let themselves stop believing in rescue. They would not let themselves stop expecting rescue.

After days of almost unbelievable endurance, rescue came. It is hard to believe that the attitude of the men did not make a difference in their survival. But the point I am trying to make is that their attitude is the one to take, whatever the outcome. It is better to go down to defeat believing in victory, affirming it and striving for it to the end and helping others to strive for it to the end, than to go down believing in defeat, expecting and submitting to it.

Faith leads human beings to try all sorts of things, some that they fail at. We can be grateful for this—for many of those who failed at first have gone on to win ultimate victory or prepare the way for others to win it. And only those who have dared to go beyond their depth have added to the stature of the human race.

Charles Fillmore believed that he would live forever. Do you think he would have lived a more useful life if at ten he had accepted the fact that he was a hopeless invalid? He lived to be ninety-four. He founded Unity and ran it. He wrote, lectured, traveled, lived actively when he was in his nineties. He influenced millions of persons.

And he taught them to believe in the good. He taught them to keep believing. He taught them to keep acting on their belief.

I wonder how many of us can continue to apply ourselves with spirit to a task once we have become convinced that we cannot succeed at it. Even the hero who stands by his post and refuses to flee although he knows he will be overwhelmed makes his stand precisely because he believes that good will come out of

69

what he is doing. He is able to make his stand because he knows, perhaps not consciously but in the deep core of his being, that he is "a part of all that's good, and good shall be victorious."

This is a knowledge that all of us have access to, and I think we know it most clearly in moments of crisis. Then our eyes are lifted to it and we catch a glimpse of the eternal Truth shining through the changing facts.

On one of the dark nights of my own spirit, I wrote this poem. I think it contains a truth:

> How much the human spirit
> Outweighs the human pain—
> So much that no experience
> But can be counted gain!
>
> What faith before impossibles
> A man is capable of
> Who, being overwhelmed,
> Yet trusts that God is love!
>
> What doubter dares to say
> Man is not god or near it
> When even his defeats become
> The triumph of his spirit!

A pessimist may ask, "How can you look at things and take a positive attitude?" But I ask, "How can you look at things and take any other?"

70

"If we had never before looked upon the earth," wrote Richard Jefferies, "but suddenly came to it man or woman grown, set down in the midst of a summer mead, would it not seem to us a radiant vision?"

Copernicus, looking at the heavens, exclaimed, "All I can do is adore!"

Someone asked William Blake, "When the sun rises do you not see a round disc of fire, somewhat like a guinea?" "Oh, no," said Blake, "I see an innumerable company of the heavenly host crying, 'Holy, holy, holy is the Lord God, the Almighty.'"

Oh, the unbelievable, unexplainable, fantastic, marvelous world! Too vast, too varied to be comprehended with all our sense and senses! And most marvelous of all the marvels, the human being!

As I have said, one of the oldest and most universal of stories is the story of the baby born to a king who in one way or another is taken from the palace and brought up as a woodchopper or a swineherd or in some other lowly position. Then, when he is grown, he makes his way back to the palace, and there finds out that he is not a woodchopper but a king's son. And immediately that is what he is. Because the truth is that that is what he always was. He is a king's son; he merely believed he was a woodchopper; and he has only to see the truth to come into his birthright.

This is what the positive thinkers believe about all of us. We look at human beings and see the woodchopper, but we also see the king's son. We look at the world

71

and see the facts and flaws, but we also see the divine perfection working to come forth.

Down through the centuries there have been many to say, "It won't work." "Nothing good can come out of this." "It's hopeless." Even, "The world is coming to an end."

Yet after thousands of years of chance and change, we are still pursuing the great and unpredictable adventure that is life; there are more of us than there have ever been; we are healthier, more intelligent, more understanding, more generous, more human-hearted.

I wonder how much the human race has ever been helped by those who pointed out the dreadful state of affairs. Suppose they were right. Whom would you want at your side in the mine disaster? One of them, prophesying destruction? Or someone with courage, faith, and hope, someone with a cheerful word and a friendly hand on your shoulder in the dark, trying to find a way out and helping you to find your way out too?

A friend of mine won a citation in World War I because when the engineers he was with were pinned down on a hillside by enemy fire, he kept them singing while they worked.

Singing under fire! Whispering to a downcast friend in a mine disaster all the reasons you can think of why he will be rescued! Pollyanna foolishness! Surely, but it is out of such brave and wonderful human foolishness that human progress and endurance have come.

Thank God for the ones with a word of cheer, a smile of encouragement, a thought of hope! Thank God that in times of trouble most of us become pollyannas, believing in the good, seeking the good, and helping others to believe in it and seek it. If this were not so, the human race would have vanished long ago—obliterated not by events but by its own discouragement.

As I have written somewhere—at least, I should have written it—I may not know who will win the race, but I do know who will lose it—it will be the one who loses faith and gives up.

Never lose faith. Never give up.

If in the end the world comes tumbling down, I hope I shall hear, across the tumult of the falling stars, some Roland of that unimagined age blowing his deathless horn at Roncesvalles, blowing his defiance of all that is less than might have been, blowing his faith that the good will triumph yet.

And if I am there, I pray that I will put my horn to my lips, too, and blow my note of courage for my friends to hear and take heart by.

You Are Not Alone

There are times when we all feel alone. We have things to meet and we feel we have to meet them alone. But we do not have to meet anything alone. God is with us.

God is with you. Yes, God! You do not have to face your problems alone. You do not have to make your overcomings alone. There is One with you always who will help you in everything you have to meet.

This does not mean that you do not have to make any effort yourself. You have to make all the effort of which you are capable. You have to determine to see the problem through, and you have to devote your energy and intelligence to handling it. But you do not have to depend on your own resources alone. You have access to God. If we felt that we had only our own resources to depend on, we might feel discouraged indeed, for often when we have a struggle to make, we do not seem to have much to struggle with. The qualities of heart and mind and body that we need do not seem to be there. But if we hold on, if we do not lose heart but persist in effort and prayer, we may find that we have qualities we never guessed we had, God's qualities.

You may feel that you have no awareness that God is with you. If this is so, you can develop it. How can you develop it? You can develop it through prayer. It may come immediately. It may come slowly. But if you consciously and persistently seek the presence of God, you will find that presence.

This seeking does not have to be laborious. Regular periods of prayer are helpful if you have the time and the desire for them; but best of all is this: Throughout the day remind yourself that God is with you. On waking, on sitting down to breakfast, on leaving the house, on starting to work, on taking up a new task, on meeting anybody, on discussing a problem, on starting out in the evening, on lying down to sleep, remind yourself that God is with you. Whenever you feel that you need strength or freedom or wisdom or peace, remind yourself that God is with you, helping you.

In this way you will come to know that truly God *is* with you. You will come to feel His loving, living presence. This does not mean that something phenomenal will happen. God is Spirit. He is intelligence, love, life. And you will feel His presence as a quickening of your intelligence, love, and life. You will feel Him as a new sense of assurance and peace such as you never had before. You will feel Him as a new ability to meet and master problems. He will make Himself manifest to you not in a strange and mysterious way but as better health, as a more alert mind, as increased harmony with others, as greater success in your affairs.

Do not be discouraged if you do not see instant results. Have patience with yourself. If you think of yourself as weak or inadequate or unworthy, if you let the burden of past mistakes bear you down and believe you are a failure, truly you will find it hard to succeed. Remember there probably never was anyone who always succeeded the first time he tried. As I have said, scientists may fail hundreds, even thousands of times before they finally succeed. Success is often the result of patient persistence through failure.

Many persons have to build a consciousness of the presence of God thought by thought as one builds a house brick by brick. It does not matter if you are not able to build the entire edifice in a day. *It is accepted according to that a man hath, and not according to that he hath not.* The important thing is that you keep trying. *And ye shall seek me, and find me, when ye shall search for me with all your heart.*

Know that God is with you right now, this minute, helping you to meet the present need. Put out of mind yesterday's regrets, tomorrow's fears. It is right now that God is with you, and you have only one thing to meet—the present moment. God is with you as you meet it!

God is always willing to help us, but sometimes we do not let Him help us until we have exhausted all our resources. Someone who does not know how to swim exhausts and frustrates himself in aimless struggles. If he would relax and float, he would discover that the water would support him, and with intelligent effort he could get to shore. Sometimes we struggle until we are nearly exhausted before we are willing to relax and let

God support us. Then we make the astounding discovery that He does support and sustain us, and with a little intelligent effort we reach the shore!

And often success is nearer than it seems to be. Sometimes where no visible results appear, a great work has been done in the invisible. *Fear not ... for from the first day that thou didst set thy heart to understand ... thy words were heard.* The work of God is largely done in the invisible; it is a spiritual work done on heart and mind. But it is no less real because it is invisible.

So if you should come to the point where you feel like giving up, it is then you must hold on. Hold then steadfastly to the thought that God is with you and keep steadfastly on. For it is then, even in that moment, that the victory may appear.

For God is with you, your certitude of victory. He does not forsake you. He loves you. He sustains you. He will help you up. He will help you on. He will help you to assurance in yourself.

God is with you! That is the truth. Keep it before you. Think it, affirm it, repeat it until you have fixed it indelibly on your mind and heart, until you feel it in the inmost fiber of your being. You will feel it. Be sure of that. You will feel it so clearly that you will never doubt it again. Then nothing you have to meet will ever seem overpowering again, for you will know that with you is something infinitely more powerful than any negative belief, something braver than any fear, stronger than any weakness, firmer than any wavering, wiser than any doubt. You will know that in you is the divine capacity to meet every situation, the wisdom to know what should be done, and the strength to do it. You will know—and knowing, you will never be alone again—that with you is God!

The Evolution of the God-Idea

What is God?

We use many terms when we speak of Him.

God is Principle, we say. Or, God is Father. We speak of the Christ. Or we say that God is incarnate in Jesus Christ. We speak of Divine Mind as God. Or we say that His name is Jehovah. He is the One; yet we speak of the Trinity of God.

God does not change. God is eternally the same. But the God-idea changes. The God-idea changes as we human beings change. Your God-idea changes as you change.

God is that which rules the world. What do you believe rules your world? What do you trust in? What do you depend on for your help?

You probably cannot give a simple answer. At different times you have thought of God in different ways, and all these different thoughts are mixed together in your mind.

The truth about God is the highest kind of truth we can know. It is a many-faceted truth, like a diamond. Solid geometry does not make the truths of plane geometry less true. It just adds another dimension to the truth. So it is with God. New concepts of Him do not mean that older concepts are no longer true. They are still true—only they are not enough.

The earliest notion of what rules the world must

have been not so much a sense of God as a sense of impersonal force, the presence of power, a pervading influence.

God may be thought of as force. Certainly the first human beings lived in a world ruled by force. The seasons rolled over them; winds blew; rain and sun beat down; storms raged; beasts and men attacked one another.

In such a world human beings needed courage; they sensed God's presence most clearly in the hero. To set force in motion, force is needed; so prayer became a magic rite or spell. The magician did not ask the gods for favors; he sought to compel the power that rules the world.

To many of us, God is still force, largely. We depend on force to achieve our ends.

And force is good, force is necessary. Without it nothing gets done.

But force is not enough.

For one thing, we cannot set a force in motion without setting an equal force in motion in the opposite direction. This is Newton's Third Law of Motion. The ancients called it the Law of the Opposites. When we live on the level of force, we are always setting into motion forces that are opposite to what we want. For force is not good or evil. The fire gives warmth, but also it burns; it works to create and destroy.

To believe that the world is ruled by force is the most primitive of all beliefs. It is the belief of brutes. And human beings are not brutes. The belief in force is not enough for human beings.

God may be thought of as force, but God is a force that acts like a person. It was not long before human beings began to personify the divine force.

God never puts Himself out of reach. He is a force to those who need to rely on force. He is a person to those who need to depend on Him as a person. And probably all of us have times when we long to know God as a person. Because we are persons.

You are a person. Around you are persons. You understand them. You feel that they understand you. You know how to communicate with them. When you call, they will hear and may respond.

It is hard not to imagine God like ourselves. We want to make a statue or paint a picture of Him. We say, "He is," not, "It is." We say, "Our Father,"—or even, "Our Mother"—and immediately the mysterious reality we are yearning to identify ourselves with seems close and real.

When God is thought of as a person, He becomes the king and ruler of heaven and Earth, to whom we owe absolute obedience. He may incarnate as an avatar or personal savior. Prayer becomes supplication; for, if a personal God desires, He may set aside the rules by which His world is run; at least, we can plead with Him to do this for us.

But in most religions based on the idea that God is a person, He usually has become not only a loving

Father but a stern judge. The world turns at His will—He made it and He may destroy it. He demands sacrifices, even of life, and He may punish disobedience to His will with harsh and everlasting judgments.

To think of God as a person is good when it makes us feel that we understand Him. It is a step toward God. But it is not enough.

God is not made in our image. We are made in His image. Between these two views there stretches an infinity. Our aim must be ultimately not to see God as a person but to see ourselves in our godlikeness.

God may be thought of as a person, but God is a person that acts like law.

Today most educated people believe that the world is ruled by law. This is the age of science; as scientific knowledge increases, we see that what we once thought was ruled by force and chance is really ruled by law.

Apollo, the willful and beautiful god, is metamorphosed into a glowing, incandescent globe nearly 93 million miles away; we put its energies to work for us. Rain and drought are not the whim of Jupiter or Thor, but the result of natural laws at work in the atmosphere; we can predict the weather and one day will control it. The tides are obedient not to Neptune, but to the pull of gravity; we make our plans to harness them. Even the behavior of living creatures and of human beings, we come to see more and more, is subject to laws. These laws, too, we can learn and use.

Religions that conceive of God as law often think of themselves as sciences more than as religions. God becomes impersonal Principle, and life is governed by the law of cause and effect, of sowing and reaping. Ignorance is at the root of human suffering; knowledge will be mankind's salvation. Prayer becomes affirmation—not to change the divine Principle but to change thinking so that the Truth of God may be demonstrated. Such are the teachings of the new metaphysical movements, and they grow in influence as people come to feel that life is based on law.

The oracles of this new age are the sage and the scientist. The miracles are the miracles of law. And what miracles law works—so many we no longer call them miracles! We just accept the working of the law. We touch a button and our house is instantly flooded with warmth and light. We touch another button and there before our eyes is an event taking place thousands of miles away. We fly through the air and rocket across heaven. We bring the dead to life and keep the living from dying; in a generation we have doubled the life span. And we are only at the beginning of the Age of Law.

We have hardly begun to explore the laws of mind-action. When the science of mind is as advanced as the material sciences, we shall see works beside which the achievements of today—the rockets, the atomic power, the discoveries in medicine—will seem insignificant.

For the power in the atom is insignificant beside the

power in the mind. We cannot even envision what we shall achieve as the science of the human potential unfolds, as we learn how to focus and direct the powers of the mind. Here we stand only on the shore. A few persons have landed and come back and reported. "There is an unknown world here!" they exclaim, and bring back to us more dazzling tales of treasures and marvels to be found in us than ever Columbus or Ponce de Leon or stout Cortes brought back to the rulers of Spain.

Yet even law is not enough. A world governed by law, a world where we can always determine results if we know causes, is not a free world. To be a micromechanism in the macromechanism of the world, to be a pawn—even of God—is not enough. To have meaning, we have to be free.

Those who think that the world is ruled by law have won great triumphs—they have changed the lives of all of us—and they will win greater triumphs yet. But law is incomplete. Though it illumines our minds, it does not fire our hearts. To live we need more than light, we need warmth.

For God may be thought of as law, but God is a law that acts like love.

When we look at the world, it is hard for most of us to believe that love made it. But the time will come when it will be as natural for us to think that love made the world as it is now for us to think that force and chance made it, if we are atheists, or that a superperson made it, if we are fundamentalists, or that law made it, if we are scientists.

We have emerged from the time when God seemed most like force. We are emerging from the time when God seems most like a person. We have entered the time when God seems most like law. The time when God seems most like love is still to come.

But it is coming. Here and there, now and then, persons appear who have outstripped the rest of us. They are, as it were, mutations on the tree of life. They show us what the human race is moving toward.

The God-idea as force produces the hero. The God-idea as a person produces the savior. The God-idea as law produces the sage. The God-idea as love produces the Christ, the innate divinity in all of us.

Only a few human beings have tried to live as if God were love. But even though we do not yet live this way ourselves, we sense that this is the way we are intended to live.

Most of us have moments when we live by love. For a moment we put off selfishness. For a moment we are not concerned with getting, but with giving. For a moment our thought is all for others. Such moments may be moments of pain—sometimes it takes pain to push us beyond ourselves. We may be reluctant; we may be frightened. Yet we sense that somehow at such moments we have lived more deeply, more intensely, more meaningfully than at any other time in our lives.

For a moment we have entered into a new dimension of life, living not as we live most of the time, bounded by the horizons of self, but as we are intended to live in a world where the horizons are of love.

Most of us manage to love one or two—our wives, our sons, our fathers, our sisters, a friend—and this little love makes the difference between bare existence and life for us. If loving one or two makes the difference between emptiness and purposeful life, what would life be like if we could love a hundred—or a thousand—or ten thousand—or the whole human race?

We see what such a life is like when we look toward the Master Jesus whose life, whose death, and whose life-after-death are the work of love. This is the God of love, who loves us so much that He takes on our humanness to help us put on His godliness. He suffers our faults so that we may enjoy His perfection. He lets Himself endure the appearance of death so that we may know the reality of life.

When we come to Him hungry for food, He breaks the bread and fishes and feeds our bodies. When we come to Him hungry for God, He breaks the bread of Himself and feeds our spirits. When we bring Him our sick and dead, He gives them life. When we bring Him our sinners, He writes in the sands of life: "Your sins are forgiven you. Go and sin no more."

He is the embodiment of divine force—and in Him we see that the force of God is the power of love that heals and frees and supplies our needs. He is God as a person, and in Him we see that the face and voice of God are the face and the voice of love. We have only to touch the hem of His garment and we are healed. He is the fulfilling of the law, and in Him we see that the law is fulfilled by love.

When we believe that God is love, we love. That is all. When we love, we give—ourselves and all we have.

We love those we love out of the joy of giving, with no thought of return. We do not love them because they love us. We do not love them because they are good. We do not love them because it is pleasant and easy to love.

We stand by them in their pain. We stand by them in their shame. We stand by them when they make deep and hard demands on us.

And we are transformed!

We see the world with the eyes of love, and how different life looks! We do not make demands for ourselves, but upon ourselves. Love demands that we rise to our highest potential; as we do, we live to our highest potential. We may not find an easy life, but we find a great life. As we give to our utmost, we live to our utmost.

Why am I afraid of love?

Where need I seek shelter who have found love? May I not trust in love to feed me and clothe me? Will love not keep my going out and my coming in? May I not lay my head in the heart of love and sleep?

This is the way Jesus lived. This is the way the Christ in us bids us to live. To live by love is still too hard for most of us, but the central figure of our faith is this God-man who is love. Today love is only the leaven. But tomorrow it will be the whole loaf.

God may be thought of as force, but God is a force that acts like a person.

God may be thought of as a person, but God is a person that acts like law.

God may be thought of as law, but God is a law that acts like love.

God may be thought of as love—and beyond love?

Beyond love lies the infinite, range on range. But now even the peaks of love lie hidden in the mists.

For now it is enough to say, God is love.

A Conversation with a Mayfly

One day as I sat thinking about the world and what it might mean, a mayfly blew against my window, clung there, delicate, translucent, trembling, frail, rose, was caught by a passing breeze, and in a moment vanished.

"This world," I thought, "is vast and varied, crowded from endless end to endless end with countless marvels, all unaccountable, different, and strange. If this world has a Maker, whatever made it must be—whether Being or Principle—far above me, not only in power but in intelligence. And that being the case, it must also be far above me in love; for such an intelligence would not leave itself loveless.

"But here is this mayfly, which lives only for a day, making winged love and fluttering on the summer breeze, and falls into a fish's mouth. Not even I, unloving as I am, would make a world where creatures are born to live a day, suffer, and die. How can a world so cruel be the work of a love so intelligent as the Maker of this world would have to be?

"How can this world have a Maker?"

Then I cried out, "O God, if there is a God, explain this to me!"

I listened. Much to my surprise, I heard an answering voice. It was not God's. The mayfly had flown back and was clinging again to my windowpane. And this little creature was speaking.

"Because I will die," said the mayfly, "would you not let me be born?"

I would have been surprised to hear God speak; I was even more surprised to find myself in conversation with a mayfly. I could only mutter, "What is that you say?"

"I was saying," said the mayfly, "that it is true that I live only for a day, fluttering on the summer breeze and making winged love, and shortly fall into a fish's mouth. But because I will die, would you not let me be born?"

"Oh, that's not what I meant at all," I said.

"Then what did you mean?" said the mayfly.

"Why, I would have had you born to be something much . . . I would have had you born to be . . . . " Suddenly I was not sure just what I was going to say. "It's hard for me to say," I said. "But I would have made you different. Yes, wonderfully different!"

"I was afraid of that," said the mayfly.

"I wouldn't have made you such a delicate, frail creature, so easily destroyed. I'd have made you sturdy, strong, impervious to time and attack, able to survive for many years."

"And just how would you have accomplished that?" said the mayfly, fluttering its diaphanous wings. "Would you have made me, say, like a big, clumsy beetle, or perhaps like a fish even bigger and scalier than the fish you would protect me from? Or . . . no, I have it! Like a snapping turtle, with a heavy shell and a horny beak! They live a very long life, I hear. But I don't think I'd like that."

"Well, I certainly wouldn't have made you what you now are," I said. "I couldn't conceive of making something with such a little time to live—and even that little time so fraught with peril."

"Time? What is time?" said the mayfly. "Have you ever heard me complaining that I have too short a time?"

"I've never before even heard you," I said.

"If you had," said the mayfly, "you would not have heard me talking about time. It is you who are always talking about time. And yes, complaining about it. You are always early or late. You have too little or too much. You are wistful about the past and apprehensive about the future. As for me, I do not creep like you from what has been to what will be. I only waft from now to now."

The mayfly fluttered into the air, let the passing breeze waft him upward, wafted through a series of somersaults, and gently wafted back against the windowpane. "Have you ever thought what it's like to be a mayfly?"

"As a matter of fact," I said, "it's because I was thinking of what it's like to be a mayfly that I got into this discussion. I was saying to myself that I couldn't see how, in a meaningful world, a creature could be made to live for a day and be gobbled up by a fish."

"Is that all you are capable of thinking of," said the mayfly, "how I live for a day and am gobbled up? That's like saying that to be a human being is to live for seventy years and then die in bed. I think that's a very small part of the affair.

"If you could feel what it's like to spread wings—and wings like gossamer!—and feel a sudden eddy of air ripple through your soul and lift you up, up, hardly more than air yourself—but what's the use! I should be smart enough to realize you are far too heavy and gross ever to imagine what it might be like to be impalpable me."

I did not like being thought of as gross and unimaginative, but before I could think of a fitting reply, he rushed on. "You have a hard time even putting yourself in the experience of another human being, let alone another species. Oh, you observe what happens, but only as if it were happening to you. You observe, but you don't experience. You may take me apart, but you can't put me together, because you never look at me from the inside out, but only from the outside in. You never ask what it's like being a mayfly to a mayfly. You only ask what it's like to a human being."

"But your life is brief!" I said.

"To you—or to me?" said the mayfly. "And however that may be, I've never heard that life is to be measured by how long it lasts or by the way it ends."

"The fact remains, however, you have only a day. I can't believe there's anyone who wouldn't agree that's

94

a pretty sorry lot."

"You say so," said the mayfly. "But let me ask again, when was it you heard us mayflies complain about our lot?"

The mayfly's attitude was beginning to annoy me. I thought to myself, "This sorry little creature not only has a sad and short existence, it hasn't even enough intelligence to complain about its sorry fate." Then I said aloud: "I was complaining for you. You may accept your fate, but I cannot. In fact, you make me doubt that there is any meaning in the world at all. I can't see how a God could create such a cruel and meaningless existence as a—as—"

"As a mayfly's?" finished the mayfly. "Cruel and meaningless to whom? Not to me, certainly. I find my existence very meaningful to me. And I have never heard of any commandment from God or any law of nature that decrees I must be meaningful to you.

"From what omniscient mountaintop, O man, do you decide that my dainty, amorous moment drifting on the summer wind has less meaning than your belabored, thought-tormented journey? With what measure, tell me, do you measure my misery or delight?"

"Forgive me, dear little mayfly," I said. "I'm not belittling mayflies. I'm just using you mayflies to make my point. It's the world I'm questioning—and myself. For seeing you, I suddenly saw that we are, alas, all mayflies in a mayfly kind of world!"

"As to our all being mayflies," said the mayfly,

"forgive me, dear little man, but I can think of nothing that so little resembles a mayfly as you."

"I just meant that in a general sense," I said. "I was trying to make the point that such a mayfly kind of world seems hard to explain in terms of a loving Maker."

"You aren't making general sense or any sense at all," said the mayfly. "It is only a world that is not a mayfly world which I find hard to explain in terms of a loving Maker."

"You don't understand what I'm trying to say, do you?" I said.

"You don't understand what you are trying to say, do you?" said the mayfly.

Now I had reached the end of my patience with this insect.

"You poor little mayfly," I said condescendingly. "As you have said, you are a mayfly and I am a man. 'Ah, the pity of it, the pity of it, imago!' " I was pleased with my twist on Shakespeare's line; in case you don't know, a mayfly is an imago.

"Shakespeare, isn't it?" said the mayfly. "From Othello, and badly out of context! 'Pity no more would be, were all as happy as we.' That's Blake, and much more appropriate to our discussion."

I was beginning to feel a little ridiculous debating the meaning of things with a mayfly, even one that read poetry, and it irritated me greatly to see him thinking he could outquote me.

"You poor little *ephemeroptera ephemeridae*, I do pity you!" I said.

"It is you who have named me that. But then, you call yourself *homo sapiens*," said the mayfly, and I thought I heard it tittering under its antennae. "As to my proper name, it might surprise you to know that it is Sir Dalliance O'Day, Lord of the Eternal Moment, though some of my friends call me Lover Boy.

"You will never learn, I suppose, that your names are only your own way of looking at things, and no one else's. Certainly not a mayfly's—or God's. But enough of this. If I am an ephemerid, I am too ephemerally wise to waste my day in futile metaphysical argument.

"And I have a rendezvous. Her name is Lady Sans Souci, but I call her Saucy. That's more appropriate, too."

The mayfly flew into the air, but a gust caught him and blew him hard against the wall. I cried out, but quickly saw that he was unhurt.

"I say, old top, you are capable of pity! I'm glad to see that," said the mayfly, righting himself with a shimmer of flower-petal wings. "But think about that. Shall you be capable of pity, and that which made you not feel pity, too? You can feel love—yes, even for someone as different as I; does that not say enough about your Maker?"

With a carefree dip and swoop, he went bobbing off out of sight, but before he vanished I caught the faint sound of his voice drifting back on the wind: "Because

I will die, would you not let me be born?"

Then I heard a chorus of voices. I thought I could hear the voice of every living thing, of all that crawls and flies and swims and burrows, all that hunts and is hunted, all that pounces and is pounced upon; and all these voices cried as one: "Because we will die, would you not let us be born?"

Then I heard the mountains and rivers and oceans, and even the Earth and sun and all the stars, and they all cried as with one voice: "Because we will crumble and pass away, would you not let us have our mayfly moment drifting in the wind?"

Then I heard my own voice saying, "And you, because you will die, would you rather have not been born?"

I thought about this. I thought how I have sometimes wearied of life and sometimes been overwhelmed by pain and terror, and how at such times I may have cried out, "Would that I had never been!"

But I wondered if that is what I really wished. Not to suffer this moment, not to endure this pain, not to face this uncertainty—this I can wish. But to wish I had never been born—this I can wish only because I *have* been born. Because I have been, because I am, I may wish not to be. But had I never been?

To be, even for a moment! Besides this, is there anything that means so much, anything that even means? For the living may wish to die and what is may wish not to be, but what is not can have no wish; it cannot wish to be or not to be.

Then I had a vision of God, and I thought I heard Him saying, "Go and be what is yours to be, mountain if you are mountain, human being if you are a human being, mayfly if you are mayfly." I saw all the infinite variety of things swarming forth—the things for the moment and the things for the millennia, the things known and the things unknown, the things imaginable and the things unimaginable. And I saw them all experiencing what is theirs to experience in order that they might be what they are.

I heard the Infinite Creative Force declaring, "Let there be!" I saw the Infinite Creative Force filling emptiness, forming the world, willing into being all the things that will to be, bringing forth out of the infinite nothing all the infinite somethings.

And I felt the Infinite Compassion embracing each thing as it went forth to be itself, each a unique, special, never-to-be-duplicated experience, with whatever experiences being what it was might call for.

Then I saw that a mayfly's being a mayfly demands certain risks and perils and anxieties and agonies. And likewise a mountain's being a mountain, and a human being's being a human being.

If the mayfly is to be a mayfly, it must suffer these risks and perils and anxieties and anguishes. But if to be what I am, I must be born just outside a hungry fish's mouth, will I not hope for a plenitude of fish? If I am a mayfly, will I not pray for a mayfly world? If I am a mayfly . . . ah, to be a mayfly! What else in all the world can be so meaningful, so desirable—if I am a mayfly!

I saw that each thing suffers and dies, but each has the unique experience of being itself, something exquisitely original and special, living a life nothing else has ever lived or ever will. And it is because each creature is the unique, original, and special thing it is that it has meaning. My meaning rises from the fact that I am not you, but I am myself.

Then I saw around me all the infinite host of living things, and I heard them singing, each one in a different voice, but all as with one thought:

"Thanks be to the Compassion so creative and the Creativity so compassionate that it has made it possible for me to be me, whatever that may be like and whatever that may call for."

And I lifted my voice in song and sang my praises, too.

The Seed and the Harvest

When I was a small child, I thought of God as a gigantic figure, bearded and stern, lurking up in the sky somewhere, peeping down from behind a cloud to check on what I was doing. He had a huge black book in His hand in which He kept a careful tally of all my misdeeds, which to my small boy mind were numerous. There are many people in the world, I imagine, who have such a notion of God, perhaps not quite so childish but unpleasantly similar.

We often speak of the law of sowing and reaping as if it were one of the incontrovertible laws that control the universe. It hangs over many human beings like a dark cloud, turning this world and the next into an eternal prison house, where a divine Mikado makes the punishment fit the crime.

But God is not a heavenly bookkeeper. This is a just world, and we are accountable; but there is much more to the world than keeping accounts or weighing a life in the balance.

The law of sowing and reaping is at best a part truth.

I am a gardener. As a gardener I have learned several great truths about sowing and reaping.

The first of these is that we never reap what we sow.

Early in spring, usually around the first of March, I go out to the garden plot I have prepared, and I take with me a handful of small round hard brown pellets

101

about half the size of BB's. These are almost always the first thing I sow in spring. I draw a furrow, drop the little pellets into the furrow, and cover them with earth. But I do not expect to reap small round hard brown pellets half the size of BB's, though once in a while that is about all I get. What I expect to reap is something entirely different. I expect to reap fat round red radishes, juicy and crisp when I bite into them. And this is what I do reap—not hard brown pellets, but fat red radishes. I do not reap what I sowed, but something deliciously different.

I take a handful of fine dust and I sprinkle it across the earth. That fine dust is what I sow. But I reap not a sprinkle of dust, but a whole summer of beautiful red petunias, months of bloom. That is what I reap.

No matter what I sow in my garden, not once do I reap what I sowed, but always something so different that if I did not know it grew from what I had sown, I could not imagine a connection. Neither lettuce nor lily looks like its seed.

Not only in a garden is it true that we do not reap what we sow, but it is true in every area of life.

We sow a thought, and we reap not a thought but a poem. Or we may reap a story, or a book, or an invention. Some have sown a thought and reaped millions of dollars.

We sow a prayer and we reap not a prayer but health, not a prayer but supply, not a prayer but freedom, not a prayer but new directions. How often I have seen this in Silent Unity.

We sow a dream, and we may reap a whole new world. From a dream, some human beings have reaped a new way of life for the whole human race. Perhaps you who read this have sown a dream or a prayer or a thought, and you can testify what may be harvested from such a seed.

When life gives you seed to sow, of this I am sure, the one thing it does not expect back from you is the seed it gave you to sow.

The Bible makes this plain, Jesus tells of a master going on a journey who calls his servants to him, entrusts to one five talents, to another two talents, and to the third one talent. On his return, he demands a reckoning. The first servant gives him back not five talents, but ten. The second gives him back not two, but four. The master praises them, *Well done, thou good and faithful servant. . . . unto every one that hath shall more be given.* But the third servant had merely buried his talent in the earth. When he digs it up and gives it back, the master snatches it from him, and gives it to the first servant. He throws the third servant out of doors, crying, *Thou wicked and slothful servant!* so that even the little he had was taken from him.

God gives us much for our little, but He expects much from us, too. God is the great creative force of love. That force of love sows its seed all over the universe, and has sown its seed since the beginning of time. That is why we are here, all of us.

Love sows its seeds, and expects them not just to re-produce but to proliferate and become all the infinite variety of living forms. Love and life never expect to reap what they sow but always something more, even something that will beget yet more again.

This is the first great truth about sowing and reaping.

The second truth that I have gleaned from my gar-den is this: In this world, if we sow a radish seed, we usually get a radish, but also we get weeds.

This is not only a flowery world; it is also a weedy world. Someone has said, "If you want to be a gar-dener, it is not enough to love flowers, you have to hate weeds."

I do not always hate weeds. I even have a sneaking admiration for them; they survive where nothing else will. I have prayed, "Let me be the human weed of God!"

The dictum that we reap what we sow draws a pic-ture of a neat and orderly world that is not the kind we live in. We might reap what we sow if we lived in a laboratory, though from what I have read about scien-tists and their experiments it is not unusual for them to find surprises there. But our world is not a labora-tory world; it is a world of life, even a teeming world. There is no bare crack that will not soon be crowded with living, proliferating forms.

This is a varied world, streaked and spotty, full of twists and turns, full of surprises, an original world, a creative world, one where we are expected to be creative, too. We cannot just bury our talent in the hope that one day we can go out and dig it up. We may find that even the little we had has been taken away from us; sometimes we sow and reap nothing.

I have sown a row of beans and gotten not a single one; the rabbits chewed them off right to the ground. If we want to have beans, we have to do something about rabbits—and all the other nuisances that are likely to keep us from ever enjoying a tasty dish of them.

We have to have courage. I have often marveled at the courage it takes to be a farmer. He has to gamble with the chancy weather of this spinning world.

We have to have faith, for we plant in one season and we reap in another, and the winds will shift many times between these two events.

We have to have good judgment. I have not infrequently tried to plant things that would not grow in the place and season in which I tried to grow them.

We have to have patience. We have to be willing to let things take their natural course. I have a grandson. When he was very small, he wanted a garden, so I gave him some seed and a garden row and showed him how to sow the seed. But he never gave his seed a chance—every day he was digging and prying along that row to see if any of his seeds were coming up—and he harvested nothing at all.

We have to have diligence. There is not much we can extract from this life without a lot of hard work.

And we have to have perseverance.

In order to reap what we hope to reap in this wonderful, chancy, living, teeming, flowery, weedy world that is the world we have come up to, we have to not only sow our seed, but we have to cultivate it with courage, faith, good judgment, patience, diligence, and perseverance. Otherwise, we may reap weeds—or nothing at all.

But there is yet another great truth about sowing and reaping: I reap where others sowed.

Would this not be a bare world if each of us had to start things from their beginning and build from there?

I am the director of Silent Unity. We reach millions today because Charles and Myrtle Fillmore, May Rowland, and hundreds of others have sowed their seed of faithful prayer through more than ninety years of service.

Unity is here only because down through the centuries many people sowed many thoughts—Quimby and Emerson and Hegel and Kant and Berkeley and Servetus and Bruno and Plotinus and Plato and the great thinkers of the East and Jesus—the Fillmores reaped these centuries of wisdom and planted in their turn.

I thank God that when I want to go somewhere I do not have to invent the wheel, but can roll along on wheels that others have devised. When I am putting on my clothes, I often think of the unknown men—or women probably—who contrived the spinning of thread and the weaving of cloth. When I put on my shoes, I bless the unsung genius who tied the first bowknot; he—or she—has made life easier for every generation since.

Oh, I thank God for all the thousands and thousands of people who have sown so that now I may reap!

Even more wonderfully, sometimes we reap where no one has sown. What can we say of this except that sometimes God sows, and when He does, He does not ask the sower but appoints him and He may choose even the unlikeliest of fields in which to do His sowing. Has not the whole world come from such a sowing? God said, "Let there be!" and out of nothing, something started, something that has never ceased to grow.

But there is still another truth about sowing and reaping: I may reap where others sowed, but to live a life worth living, I must sow what is mine to sow, and to live best, I must sow with no thought of reaping.

I have always loved the little saint who, when God said, "You can have anything you ask," replied, "When my shadow falls behind me, let whatever it falls on be blessed."

What a blessed way of life—to give what is yours to give, not for worldly gain, not even to take private pride in the good you have done, but because it is yours to give. To sing not because others may applaud but because you are a singer; to work not because you will be paid for your work but because you are a worker; to sow not that you may reap but because you have seed to sow—this is the human being living at his highest pitch of creativity. Civilization is here only because so many Johnny Appleseeds of mind and spirit have wandered across the wilderness—of this Earth and of our hearts—planting their apple trees of truth and beauty, apple trees they will never eat the fruit of.

To give, to give as fully and freely as we can, not so that we will be blessed but so that life will be blessed, should this not be our highest aim?

Does not the universe set this example? Nothing in it reaps what it sows; everything gives what it has to give.

The universe does not say, "Dance and you must pay the piper," but "Dance the dance you have in you to dance!" You only pay the piper when you dance his dance, not yours.

And the universe dances to no dismal one-note tune. Its music is a medley of melodies, different but in harmony, where even the dissonances, if they are your note, merge into the magnificat of life.

There is a law of sowing and reaping. But it lies on the world not like a judgment but a promise. It is the law of creativity. And it says, Sow and you shall reap. But you shall sow what is yours to sow, that you may reap what is life's to give. For the seed is in your hand, but the harvest is in life's hand.

Sow a thought, and reap a revelation. Sow a hope, and reap a miracle. Sow a dream, and reap a new life for yourself and perhaps for all the world.

For the world is not a countinghouse but a garden. And God is not the keeper of accounts but the creative spirit of life bringing forth out of its own infinite will-to-grow its ever-renewing, ever-multiplying, ever-proliferating bounty.

Because He Is Love

Who of us does not have times when he thinks he is not good enough to go to God for help? But God does not help me because He approves or disapproves of what I am doing.

God helps me because He is God. Because He is life. Because He is love.

God does not help me because I am good.

God helps me because He is good.

God does not help me because I deserve help, or love me because I deserve love.

Do you love only those who have no flaws? And would you think that you can love where God cannot? Love sees things perfect in spite of flaws.

I do not have to be perfect to lay hold of love's perfection.

God does not answer my prayers to reward me because I have been good or deny my prayers to punish me because I have been bad.

God does not strike a bargain.

God does not work for pay.

God gives.

God does not wait until I give myself to Him to give Himself to me. He seeks me even when I flee from Him. And whither may I flee from Him who is everywhere at hand?

God has me in His heart, whether I have Him in my heart or not.

I do not have to be the most willing for Him to choose me, or the most capable for Him to use me.

It is not only good people God has used to do His good.

It is not only brave people God has used to win His victories.

It is not only righteous people God has used to establish right.

So I hold out my heart and I pray, "God, whatever my heart may have felt, love through it."

I hold out my mind and I pray, "God, whatever my mind may have thought, think through it."

I hold out my hands and I pray, "God, whatever my hands may have done, act through them."

For I know that God does not give His strength only to the strong, or His wisdom only to the wise, or His joy only to the joyful, or His blessing only to the blest.

God does not help me because of what I am.

God helps me because of what He is.

God is love.

If Your Heart Condemn You

How often do our hearts condemn us! How often do we shut ourselves out from the fullness of life with a sense of sin and wrongdoing! How often do we deny ourselves the happiness of today by refusing to let go of the shame of yesterday! How often does our conviction that we are miserable, sinful creatures keep us from our heritage as the beloved children of God!

Life should have a full, rich flavor. There should be joy in the little happenings of every day. It should be joy to feel the peace of our own being. We should find joy in love and in all the beauty with which God has surrounded us.

But often we give our thought to our own hearts' condemning, and though all God's world shouts of joy and beauty and love to be enjoyed, we will not turn from the wailing wall of our unworthiness to take in the glory and compassion.

Yet for all who suffer from a sense of sin and wrongdoing there is this freeing Truth: The will of God is not suffering and denial; the will of God is life, life exuberant, life triumphant, life exultant!

We listen to our conscience as if it were the voice of God. That of course is not true.

The accusing voice of conscience is not the loving voice of God. If we are suffering from a sense of condemnation, it is not God who is condemning us, it is we who are condemning ourselves. God is love. Our conscience is formed by our experience and training as children; it varies from culture to culture and from individual to individual. In some persons there seems to be no conscience, in others it is so exaggerated that no matter how uprightly they may live, their conscience will not let them alone; like a thief by night it comes to whisper of guilt and demand payment. But though they pay a thousand times over, conscience is not satisfied. It returns and returns again.

Can you not be as kind to yourself as you are to a stranger? If a stranger came to you and told you he was full of shame and remorse because of things he had done as a child, would you not tell him to forget and to go free? Yet are you still punishing yourself for things you did when you were a child spiritually? Surely you have punished yourself enough. Your soul has paid the price. Let it go free.

If you have injured another, it is right to make restitution if you can. But punishing yourself is not restitution. It is but adding a new wrong to an old one. Often you cannot make restitution directly to the one you have injured. But the law of life does not require this any more than it requires that you always give to the one from whom you receive. All the good you have ever done to anyone is your restitution. Does not the good you have done outweigh any evil you may have done?

We do not increase our spiritual stature by adding

114

thoughts of shame to the shame of our deed. If you stumbled while walking in the darkness, would you rebuke your foot? Or would you light a light?

The denial of life is not the will of the Creator of life. Not the one who withdraws from life but he who has faith in life and finds joy in living is a spiritual man. The spiritual man enters with exuberance into all the activities of life. He loves life. So great is his sense of livingness, so keen is his feeling of the wonder and worth of living that to him every day is a journey in jubilance. He wakes in the morning delighted to be off on the adventure of living; he extracts from each moment its utmost of pleasure and surprise; he lies down at night with a sense of contentment, at peace with himself and with the universe. He knows that pain is a sign that something is wrong; if it comes, he does not cling to it but seeks to set the wrong right.

The truth is that if we do not enjoy and cherish love and beauty and joy, we live a half life.

Love love. Love is the heart of God. Love is the way out of the prison of the self. Love is completion.

Love beauty. Beauty is but another name for God. It is the face of God as truth is the mind of God. It is the language of the spirit as truth is the language of the mind. It is the witness of God's presence in the world.

Love joy. Joy is the laughter of God. Joy is a habit and a habitation of the heart that abides in His love. What would you will for your beloved save joy? You are the beloved of God, and the love of God surpasses

115

yours. *If ye ... know how to give good gifts unto your children, how much more shall your Father which is in heaven give good things to them that ask him?*

If you do not love yourself, who are the beloved of God, is that holiness? If you do not love your body, which is the temple of God, is that holiness? You do not find God by repudiating Him in yourself. You do not honor Him by denying Him in your body and renouncing His world.

If a plant is denied its sustenance, it withers. So our soul withers when we deny it the love and beauty and joy that are its sustenance.

You would not punish a child for doing childish things. Are we not all children of God? Will He blame us because, being yet children, we do not always act with spiritual maturity?

Surely the forgiveness of God is ours even before our hearts reach out to accept it. Surely the understanding of God is ours even when we fail to understand ourselves.

God does not require of us more than we are able to give. Having given us bodies, He does not ask us to deny the needs of our bodies. Having given us the capacity for happiness, He does not ask us to repudiate happiness. Having given us the desire for love, He does not ask us to renounce love.

It is good to have high standards of thought and conduct, but it is also good to accept ourselves. We do not grow by deploring what we cannot be but by finding joy in being what we are able to be. Not being yet perfected, let us accept ourselves where we are and do what we can. *It is accepted according to that a man hath, not according to that he hath not.* We are not under the law of condemnation but under the law of love.

Has your way seemed dark? Love penetrates the darkness. Love is full of light. Has your heart seemed weak? Love understands weakness. Love is full of strength. Have you felt ashamed? Love dissolves shame. Love is merciful. As you open your heart to love, all that is less than love will fade away.

If your heart condemn you, God is greater than your heart. God is love.

Not Three Worlds But One

We all want to draw close to God.

We all want to be spiritual.

But sometimes we think that spirituality must be strange and mysterious; we think that the way to God must be long and twisted and hard.

God is love.

If the way we are going is hard, it may only mean that we have not found the right way.

Often when we think we are being deep, we are only being obscure; when we think we are being mystics, we are only being mystifying—perhaps mystifying others, perhaps ourselves.

If we think of the spiritual as strange mysteries, that is what it becomes for us, and that is the only way we can touch it.

It is almost the mark of great saints and mystics that they found Spirit everywhere.

Sometimes we are like one lost in a forest. We are looking so hard for a way out that we run unseeing by the signs that point to it.

The signs of God are all around us. We have only to accept our good.

If we look too hard, we may pass right by what we are looking for.

Many of us talk about spirit, mind, and body as if these were three separate things. They are not three things but three ways of looking at one thing.

When we start thinking of our bodies as less than spiritual and of our spirits as less than physical, we divide ourselves into fragments and turn ourselves into splinter people. Then we think of our bodies as gross and ugly and evil, and of our spirits as unreal and elusive, hard to grasp and understand.

If we would start thinking about our bodies as if they were mind and our minds as if they were body, and both as if they were spirit, we would go far toward making ourselves at one with ourselves and with God.

We lay hold of Spirit when we touch our own chin or nose or a friend's hand—when we breathe in a breath of air.

I wish we could think of all we are and all the world is in the same way we think of our hearts. We hardly know when we speak of our hearts whether we are talking about the part of us that pumps our blood or the part of us with which we feel love.

Let us confuse body and mind and spirit until we cannot tell which we are talking about, for that is how they are.

God is in my body—if He is anywhere. And my body is in God. God is in the world—if He is anywhere. And the world is in God.

In some of the most profound metaphysical treatises ever written, the Buddha and his disciples sit and discuss "the transcendental wisdom of the other shore." As they discuss, they quietly chuckle.

What are they chuckling about? Because there is no transcendental wisdom of the other shore. There is no other shore! If you see another shore, it is a sign you have not arrived.

The world of Spirit is right where you are—or it is nowhere.

Start looking for it.

In things.

In people.

In yourself.

Do not think you have to look for it in strange things. Are not the most familiar things strange enough?

If you have given Spirit strange names, call it familiar names, and you may find it in familiar things.

Call it sunrise—and see that it is light and warmth.

Call it stars—and see that it is God shining through into our world.

Call it work—and see that it is losing yourself in productive activity.

Call it play—and see that it is finding yourself in the grace of joy.

Call it love—and see that it is giving yourself away. Give yourself to the least—and you find that He who is the most will give Himself to you.

Call it a little child—and you may hold God in your arms.

Call it your neighbor in need—and you may hold God in your heart.

Call it a word of truth—and you may hold God in your mind.

Sometimes we imagine we are spiritual only when we are on our knees saying prayers or when we are sitting in silent meditation.

But spirituality is no more the folded hands of prayer lifted to God than it is the straining hands of work outstretched toward our fellow human beings.

Zarathustra, one of the great mystics of all time, said: *He who sows the ground with diligence acquires more religious merit than he could gain by a thousand prayers in idleness.*

As for me, prayer is all entangled in creative thinking.

I find it hard to tell when listening stops and hearing begins.

How do I separate the rests from the music? The rests and the music flow together into one song.

Prayer may be silent meditation.

But prayer is also a word fitly spoken.

Prayer is also loving work freely done.

Everything is spiritual.

There are not three worlds but one.

When we realize this, all that we think and say and do becomes a prayer—and every prayer flowers into action.

Where does flesh end?

Where does spirit begin?

Where do I end?

Where does God begin?

The river is the river at its source. The river is the river where it flows into the sea.

Am I less spirit at my fingertips than at my heart?

Am I less mind in my feet that pick their way nimbly over rocks than in the convolutions of my brain?

O God, I am like moonlight, and You are the sun!

Can the moonlight ever be other than the sun's reflection?

Immortal Journey

What am I? What am I doing here? Where am I going?

I have a print by the Spanish artist Goya called El Colosso, the Colossus. A huge naked brute of a fellow is sitting on a log looking up at the moon and stars, his face full of question. Many times I have felt like El Colosso.

Emerson said, *What I have seen teaches me to trust my Creator for what I have not seen,* and for the most part I have been content to do that. Life has brought me up to here. For all its aches and challenges, I have found it livable and sometimes even lovable. As to where I came from, and where I am going after this life, I have not worried much as to particulars.

Personally, I find it impossible to accept the traditional notions about heaven and hell. Heaven and hell are real enough as states of mind—I have known people in both. But to believe in hell as an actual place where living souls are tortured eternally, you have to believe in a crueler God than I believe it possible for Him to be.

I once had a vivid vision of hell. I was outraged at the thought that the God of love whom I love could create such a place. But as the demon dragged me down into it, he said, "You don't have the right idea about this place. It's only here because you need it. If you'll look around, you'll see there is no one here except the people you think ought to be here."

As to heaven, I pray that we may one day attain it, but perfect bliss would require utter selflessness and perfect love. It is pretty obvious that if we should get into it now, heaven would not long stay heavenly.

Whatever else life—present or future—may contain, it must contain change. The one essential element in life, the element that makes life alive, is change. To be what you and I are, here or elsewhere, is to change— and hopefully, to grow.

I believe we are immortal beings.

I am immortal, I aver,

For I must live as if I were.

Everyone feels immortal. The psychiatrist, Karl Menninger, has said: *No human being can in the deepest core of his nature conceive of nonexistence or imagine it occurring to him.*

Life does not make sense if this is all the life there is. It is too unjust, and I believe in a God who is just. Even more, He is justice. He is law. He is even the law that is love.

Hundreds and hundreds of persons have had experiences that have convinced them that life goes on beyond this one. Such an experience is individual and subjective; you cannot make it come real to anyone who has not had it. But if you ever have one—this I know—it will be the most real thing that ever happens to you.

126

We are on an immortal journey. Children of the eternal, we are making a voyage in time, and we have come up to here.

As to the particulars of our voyage, I suppose I believe in something like reincarnation. Reincarnation seems comparatively reasonable, though personally, I don't like the word; it turns people off.

Many years ago I was studying French at the Convent of Notre Dame de Sion. The nun who taught me was a very intelligent woman, a graduate of the Sorbonne. She liked to argue with me about religion. Since the arguments were in French, I always lost. But the arguments were fun. When I brought her a piece about reincarnation, she rejected it as being utterly beyond belief. Finally I said, "What do you believe? Do you think you go sit on a cloud somewhere with a harp?" "Of course not," she said indignantly. "I believe that life is a continuous process and progress." I laughed and said, "You aren't rejecting the idea of reincarnation, you are rejecting the word, because all that reincarnation does is suggest how the process and progress may occur."

Most of the world believes in reincarnation; most of it always has. The East has always accepted the idea as the most reasonable that has ever been suggested; and though it has not been the prevailing belief in the West, thousands of famous and intelligent people from Plato and Plotinus to Edison and Einstein have believed in it.

An amazing number of people do. General Patton—
he hardly seems the type to be bowled over by mystical
notions—was absolutely convinced he had been a sol-
dier many times.

Many people, like Patton, have believed that reincarnation takes place here on Earth over and over. As for
myself, I believe God's house has many rooms in it. I
believe I have lived before. I believe I will live again.
As to where and how, perhaps it will be here—I love
this blue-green glowing globe—perhaps it will be
beyond space and even time, an inverted world where
thoughts are things and things are thoughts. But since
it will have me in it, it will not be too different, because
I cannot be too different and still be me. The essential
will remain essentially the same.

Does the thought that you have lived many times
seem strange to you? How many lives have you lived in
this one? When I was ten years old, my whole life
changed absolutely and altogether. My mother ran
away from her marriage and took me and my sister fif-
teen hundred miles from everything and everyone we
knew. Everybody who had been in my former life was
gone, except my mother and sister. And all the circumstances and conditions changed utterly.

Of my life when I was ten, or even twenty, what remains? The people who were close are scattered across
the Earth or gone from it.

When I was thirty-one I had a tremendous spiritual
experience. After agonizing soul-searching, I came to

such an illumining realization about myself, I have often told friends that I count my true birth as from that time. I went through a gate of awareness, and life on a different plane of sensitivity began.

When I was thirty-five, I lost my first wife. That was the end of a life, too; a whole new set of people and experiences came into it.

When I was fifty-five, I began yet another new life. I started to travel and speak. Since then my life experiences have altered radically again.

And I have lived these different lives, although I have lived in one city since I was ten and done one work since I was seventeen.

What about you? How many who were an important part of your life, say at twenty, are still an important part of your life? Or when you were ten? Or at your birth? Of those important to you when you were born—a very important moment—how many are important to you still? Very, very few, I would say. Even if you are very young, very few, probably.

People accompany us on this immortal journey, some for a long time and some but briefly. Their importance in our lives does not depend on how long they are with us. They can be with us for an hour—less than that, for minutes—and be transformingly important!

A few years ago I made some talks in Palm Beach. On my last day there, I spoke at a nursing home. After I made my talk, a nurse came up to me and said, "There is a woman who has asked to see you. Could you come and see her? She is very near death." She led me down a long hall and into a room where a woman lay in bed. The moment I walked into that room, I knew why I had come to Palm Beach. It had not been to make the speeches I had made. It had been because this woman had drawn me there. Don't ask me how, I don't know, but I knew that woman I had never seen before in this lifetime—I don't even know her name—as well as I have ever known anybody in this life, better than people I have known for years and years. There is no question in my mind, that woman and I for a moment had to reestablish our relationship (don't ask me what it was, I do not know, but I know that it was there and very strong) before she could go on. And so she called me to her—and I went.

People say, "I can't believe I have lived before, because I can't remember anything about those lives." But how much do you remember about this one? Very little. On this date ten years ago, where were you? I haven't the slightest idea where I was. On this date last year, where was I? I don't know. Do you know where you were? And if by accident you happen to remember the events of that particular day, do you remember where you were a week before that? Or a month before? Whom you were with and what you were doing?

And when you were ten years old, what do you remember of that year? That was one of the most eventful years in my life. But I have to think and think for a few events to dribble faintly back into my mind. And of the time when you were five? If you can recall anything, is it not usually because someone later told you it had happened?

And when we were four, three, two, one? Can we remember anything?

I have a grandson, a teenager now. When he was a little boy, we had many wonderful times together. I remember the first time I showed him the moon. Oh, he was excited! He kept pointing to it all evening long, saying, "Moon!" A short time later we were in my backyard one afternoon, and suddenly he looked up and cried, "Look, Grandpa, moon!" Sure enough, there in the sky was a pale day moon. Then he rose on tiptoe, stretched out his arms as high as he could reach, and said, "Give it to me, Grandpa!"

My grandson has already forgotten this incident and all of the other lovely, happy times we had together. If he did not live nearby, he would soon forget me, too— what I was like, at least. My grandfather was as dear to me as my grandson is, but I never saw him after I was ten, and I cannot tell you what he looked like.

One time my grandfather introduced me to Buffalo Bill. That was an occasion! But now my grandfather and Buffalo Bill and King Arthur and Robin Hood are all mixed up together in my mind. The most vivid events of my life are much like something I read in a book.

The past has an unreality about it. A mist falls between us and the past, and the mist deepens quickly, so that the figures that move in it through our minds become but phantasms, doubtful and indistinct; which is figure and which is mist becomes harder and harder to make out.

Time writes. But also it erases—almost as fast as it writes. We think of time as a rope with the events of our lives tied like knots along its length. But this is not what time is like. Time is like a bunch of keepsakes we have tossed into a drawer of our minds. There they lie tangled together. We may pull them out for a moment, but after a while we forget just when it was we threw them in.

If you have known many older people, you have probably known some who at last could not remember anything about this life. They let it all go, and slipped back, as it were, beyond their birth. I have often wondered, are they doing on this side of the door what we all must do when we pass through it?

We make our journey through time, but how strange time is. Time is important; we cannot even imagine anything happening without its taking time. But time is hard to fix or grasp. Rubbery and relative, it stretches or compresses, according to what is happening and who it is happening to and even where it is happening, conforming to all sorts of immeasurables of consciousness.

People have asked me, "If we are reborn, how long a time passes between incarnations?" I have often thought, perhaps no time at all—not in the sense of time as we mark it in the world of thoughts and things we spend this lifetime in.

Even when we are wide awake, time plays all kinds of tricks on us. A minute may be interminable; a year may flash by. Have you never waited for some joyful or some dreadful event, and counted not the seconds but the millionths of seconds? And have you never been so absorbed in some task that at last you glanced up and wondered where the day could have gone?

At night you often live in a different kind of time, the time in dreams, that has almost no relation to waking time. My friend Eric Butterworth once told me that one night he was driving a car down a country road and a hundred or so yards ahead of him he saw a stone bridge. At that moment he fell asleep, and in his sleep he dreamed a dream the events of which took days to occur. Yet he woke almost instantly, for fortunately the car had not yet even reached the bridge.

And in deep sleep, does time have any meaning to us then? If it were not for clocks and the sun, would we know that it has passed? Is it more than a bodily process? Had it not been for his long beard, would Rip van Winkle have known that he had slept for twenty years?

Time is a measure of here and now. It is futile and perhaps meaningless to ask where it has gone or when it will be.

People sometimes tell me they don't like the idea of reincarnation because they want to recognize their dear ones. So do I, and I think I will. I always have.

But how? Do I expect my grandfather to be an old man with a walrus mustache—I think he had one—who will come up to me and say, "I'm Jim Elberson." And what will I be? The little ten-year-old he knew? I don't think he would like to be that old man, and I know I wouldn't like to be that ten-year-old. And my grandmother, his wife, might like it even less. She would want my grandfather and herself to be the young couple I never knew.

No, my grandfather is never again going to be the old man he was when I knew him, nor will I ever again be that little boy. Yet I hope to see my grandfather again somewhere in my journeys. And when we meet, I think we will recognize each other. How? The same way I have recognized my dear ones in this life.

How do I recognize my dear ones? My present wife did not come to me with a sign, saying "I am your w-i-f-e." I think she knew that long before I became aware of it, but that is not the way she came. She from Louisiana, I from Delaware, came by separate, different paths, and when we met, were drawn, not by some vague recollection, but by deep inward stirrings, a feeling of oneness and love; each found the other dear—that is all.

Only blood relatives come announced, and they may or may not be dear. When you were little, your mother led you toward a big woman bending down above you, and your mother said, "This is your Aunt Agatha."

And you let out a scream and fled behind your mother's skirt.

No, dear ones don't come wearing tags or with a certain name or look. They come being dear. And that is the way we recognize them—as someone dear, close, loved. No one has to tell us. Heart speaks to heart, and that is a language all of us understand. That is the way it always has been, that is the way it will always be, that is the only way it could be.

I do not want my growth arrested anywhere. If an angel came and said to me, "Choose the happiest, most beautiful moment of your life, and I will let you stay there always," I would say to that angel, "Get thee behind me. I want to live now—always only now. I want to be alive, and to be alive is to change and to grow."

We make an immortal journey. Through chance and change, by way of worlds forgotten and courses unremembered yet graven in my soul, I came here and I journey on.

This is the human condition.

I have risen on innumerable mornings.

I have slept through innumerable nights.

I have journeyed on innumerable journeys.

I have lived in familiar and unfamiliar worlds.

I have had brave and beautiful companions, lovely friends.

I shall have them yet again.

I have been weak and strong, wise and unwise.

I have come on much curious knowledge, some remembered, some forgotten.

I have done many deeds, some worthy, some unworthy.

What I am undertaking I am not sure—but somehow I am sure it is an enterprise worthy of my effort.

Where I am going I am not sure—but I am sure it is a destination worthy of myself.

Here I am at this place on this day.

Tonight I shall lie down once more to sleep, and tomorrow I shall rise again and journey on.

The Original Look

It is as if we are on a sea voyage. We see far away what looks to be a mist take shape out of the waves. Then we see that what we took to be a mist now seems to be a mountain. As we approach yet closer we see that it is not a mountain but an island. And on still closer view, the island is seen to have many mountains, valleys, beaches, harbors, houses, wharves, roads, people, animals, trees, fields, and gardens.

And if we look at a blade of grass growing in one of these gardens—look clearly enough, keenly enough—will we not see that the grass is no more what our first careless glance considers it than the island is the mist we first took it to be?

This that seems a blade of grass will reveal itself to be an island, with its own multitudinous features as distinct and various as mountains, beaches, living creatures, fields and gardens, blades of grass. And beyond this, are there not yet further islands? Islands hardly dreamed-of, undiscovered, unexplored, unknown!

If I look outward at the heavens, the astronomers tell me that what I see as dancing points of light, the stars in the night sky, are in reality vast bodies like our sun, and may, in their turn, have around them worlds like our Earth.

One time I saw through a telescope what looked like

137

a little patch of light.

"That is the Nebula in Andromeda," said the astronomer. "This little patch of light that in the telescope looks like a puff of cotton or a bit of milkweed down, too faint to find when you take your eye from the eyepiece, is an island universe containing millions of stars, millions of suns like our own. The whole night sky sprinkled with all the stars that sparkle overhead is not so large as this puff of cotton. And this—which is almost a million light-years away—is but the nearest of myriads of such universes that astronomers have located in space."

What a world God has made!

My sense and senses shout it, and the physicists corroborate it.

Sometimes I think that physicists have more imagination than poets.

Physicists describe the world as a dance of electric particles.

The world dances!

As it dances, it sings. Had we the instruments, we could hear the harmonies.

Our world is made of light, living, singing light, dancing on its everlasting journey round the throne of the Eternal, who sent it winging on His word!

God said, "Let there be light." Having made light, what a stuff He had to make the world of.

God took the light—and was the light the movement of His thought upon the deep?—and some of the light

He made whirl in the patterns of the dance that we call matter—but it is still more light than matter. What are heaven and Earth but the momentary shape of motion?

Oh, the rainbow world we live in! Rivers of light pour everywhere, too luminous to see, showers and cascades of light. Children of light, we are ourselves the light. Swimmers in electric seas, we are ourselves the electric stuff.

This is the way God made the world.

This is the way we should see it.

It is all good. It is all beautiful. It is all extraordinary.

Nothing is plain or stale.

Nothing is inconsequential.

Nothing is to be overlooked.

How much better to mistake ordinary things to be divine than to take divine things to be ordinary!

How much better like an ancient savage to feel that a stone may be God than like a modern savant to feel that God may be no more than a stone!

Out of a clod of clay God made the first man.

All the fantastic world of living forms we see around us—what is this but clay that would not lie still? And what clay ever lies still? Behind the inert seeming, streams of electrons leap and circle in a flaming dance.

It is not enough to see God in extraordinary things. It is necessary to see that ordinary things are extraordinary, too.

Ordinary things are the house of the Beautiful.

Usual life is the fullness of living.

Every child is a Holy Infant.

Every one of us is a child of God.

Now we call a few extraordinary happenings wonders and miracles, such as the works of Jesus.

We say they are miracles because we cannot explain them and cannot duplicate them.

But what can we explain and what can we duplicate?

What is an ordinary thing?

Take a cherry tree, for instance—black boughs of winter, on those naked boughs green leaves, among those green leaves white and fragrant flowers, and when those flowers fall, red, red cherries glistening till the tree sparkles like a ruby crown, where singing birds light lightly with their songs. I have not even mentioned the taste of cherries baked in a pie! I can only say, what delightful ways God has of revealing Himself to us.

Or take the starry sky. Go out of doors tonight and look at it, the glittering night aflame with stars—not one so large as candlelight, still tapers, but with a power to move the spirit more than any summer fireworks show!

Or a baby!

Little Lord Jesus, O Holy Infant, do we need to ask You if a baby is a wonder and a miracle?

If a genie suddenly materialized, we would be struck dumb with astonishment.

We see a child, a cherry, or a star. We are delighted, but we act as if these were not as great a marvel as a genie.

We have only to look inside ourselves or step outside our door to see ten thousand wonders, each one as implausible, unexplainable, and unique as a genie.

The fact that they are wonders that happen every day does not make them less wonderful. Nor does the fact that I can sometimes correctly predict that one of them may after awhile turn into another of them—a cherry stone into a cherry tree, for instance.

I cannot duplicate a single one of them. I cannot tell you how it came to be or what it is; I cannot tell you why it is, nor can the wisest scientist.

I might say, "God!" But the word is meaningful only if you have yourself found out its meaning.

All that I can say is that I see everywhere the work of creative Spirit.

Everything God makes is an original creation. He never mass-produces anything.

He did not turn you out on a machine. You are handmade. He did not make you like anyone else.

There are more than four billion human beings. No two of them are alike. Once in awhile, almost as if in an excess of creativity—much like a grace note in a symphony—there are identical twins. But even these are different—and there are just enough of these to show that the Spirit that is at work is altogether unpredictable.

God does not create two things alike. Not two human beings. Not two cherry trees. Not two blades of grass.

When we are skillful enough to measure them, we will find that God never makes two electrons alike.

God is the infinite creativity fashioning out of His infinite thought the infinite world of force and form.

I wake in the morning and I accept this morning just as if it were like the mornings when I waked before.

How can I be so dull of perception?

This morning—like every morning—is an original creation.

Last night a freezing mist fell. This morning the world is the jewel box of God. Every tree, every bush is diamonded. Every frozen twig glitters till I hardly know whether this is ice or fire. Every tremor of the wind strikes from the crystal world blue-white and golden flames.

Today it would be hard to miss the glory. But how often we shut our eyes and complain because there is nothing to see.

We shut our ears and wonder why we never hear anything and why nobody ever has anything to say.

We never get quiet and look for God or listen for His voice, so we say that He does not exist, or if He does, He is distant and indifferent.

How long has it been since you saw the dawn? A few mornings ago I arose before the sun and saw his light come spreading across the fields. Little pink clouds formed in the sky, looking as if they might be the sun's breath misting.

How long has it been since you blew your breath on an icy morning and watched it mist?

How long has it been since you noticed how things look when there is fog? Trees and towers evaporate halfway up. You have a sense of the intangibility of things. Things are but dream-shapes drifting in your mind, and any moment may dissolve. The world is something you have only half imagined. You are detached and alone on an island of thought.

How long has it been since you walked in the half-world of moonlight, upon the bottom of the sea of night, where all things look as if they were awash in pearly tides?

How long has it been since you looked at snow, examined its star-shapes under a magnifying glass, or held out your tongue and let snowflakes melt on it as they fell?

How long has it been since you looked at frost-ferns growing on a windowpane? More mutable than grass, more delicate than flowers, blow lightly on them for a moment and they vanish.

How long has it been since you watched the lights come on in a city of an evening? the street lights blossoming along the avenues like golden flowers and the little lights in people's houses, warm, glowing squares of life?

How long has it been since you watched the people

143

pouring out of offices and factories, and felt the pulsing, surging, jostling tide of city life?

How long has it been since you sat still and looked at things by candlelight?

How long has it been since you listened to birds sing or watched them fly? I throw a few crumbs under the small tree outside my kitchen window, and to it by the dozens sparrows fly, hovering, pirouetting, twittering. Sparrows are grace in flight. Sometimes such swarms of them alight in the bare branches that I have a tree of birds. How long has it been since you looked at the bare branches of a tree? If the moon is full tonight, go out and watch it rise through the branches of a tree. The moon of winter, like a golden bird caught in a black net, will slip upward through the lacy interstices and at last soar free.

If we do not look at things, we cannot complain that life has nothing to look at. It is our look, not our lives, that becomes humdrum.

Not long ago a friend and I went for a winter hike at Unity Village. A narrow creek wanders through the back hills. The weather having been dry and cold, the water was dried up or frozen, so we could walk down in the creek bed. The banks rose high and steep above our heads, and in the meanders of this ravine we were soon altogether separated from the fields and woods above. Never farther than a few miles from home, I could not have been farther from everything familiar if I had gone ten thousand miles. The world was my usual world, but I was having an original look at it.

We walk into a familiar room and see nothing in it. We know it so well that we can find our way around in it with our eyes shut. And this is what we do.

After a while the world becomes such a room.

Have you let time's dust settle on the window? When a child finds dust on a windowpane, he writes his name in it or draws a picture. Dust, too, can disclose a world.

Things are wonderful beyond our farthest imagining. For things are God's imagining. But you are God's imagining, too. God made you in His image.

And He gave you an original look. This is the look that a child has. This is the look that God has. This is the look with which He looked at everything He had made and saw that it was good.

The Four Causes of Health

While we are taking an original look at things, let us look at a couple of subjects in these next two chapters that concern us all: The first of these is health; the second is freedom. I believe I have been granted an original look at both of these.

I have seen people healed through prayer. The first time I ever saw this was at a prayer meeting. When the meeting was over, a woman came forward, holding out her hands. "Look," she said. She was weeping. She held out her hands and slowly opened and closed them. Then she opened and closed them again.

"This is the first time in five years," she said, "I have been able to move my fingers."

Since then I have seen many people healed through prayer. I have also seen people, whom I might reasonably have expected to be healed, pray and not be healed.

But if one person ever got a healing through prayer, through changing his thinking, then there is obviously a power here that can work for all—if we learn how to use it.

If one person is healed through prayer, we can all be healed through prayer. If one person changes his life by changing his thinking, we can all change our thinking and change our lives. We have only to learn the conditions of success.

Why do we get sick? Why do we get well? Are physical explanations enough?

Aristotle—in an analysis of the way things happen in this world, an analysis that no scientist or philosopher has improved on—says that every event has four causes; these he calls the material cause, the efficient cause, the formal cause, and the final cause.

For instance, the material cause of a house may be thought of as the lumber and nails. And the efficient cause is a carpenter's hammering them together. But the formal cause is the blueprint an architect prepared. And the final cause is someone's need for shelter.

We look at a house and we ask, "How did this house happen to come into being?" If you think about this for a minute, you will see that to give an adequate answer to this question, you have to consider all four causes. Unless all four causes are operating, there will be no house.

Health and sickness, like houses and all other phenomena, have not one but four causes. Material and efficient causes cannot bring about health or sickness until the formal and final causes are in operation. There are whole groups of people whose religious beliefs forbid their accepting medical aid. Yet these people live at least as long and as healthily as others.

Material and efficient causes are the field of medical science, which has lately made marvelous discoveries in this field. But for formal and final causes, we have to look into the mind and soul. This is the field with which

Unity deals. Unity deals with the mind and soul, with consciousness, with thinking. Unity believes that when the cause of sickness in the soul is eliminated, germs are not going to attack us, any more than a carpenter is going to build a house when he does not receive an order for one from someone who needs shelter.

Eliminate the formal and final causes of a sickness and the sickness dissolves. Build in the formal and final causes of health, and health is brought forth.

What are the formal and final causes of sickness and health?

First let us consider formal causes. Unity has a great deal to say about formal causes. For the formal cause of a sickness is belief in it. People get sick because they think sickness, accept the possibility of sickness, carry around the form of sickness, as it were, in their minds.

They hear that everyone has been catching cold, and immediately they are afraid they are going to get one. In a sense, we blueprint colds just as an architect blueprints houses.

You can see that if we carry around in a pocket in our minds the blueprint of a sickness, we are much more likely to build it into our bodies than if we do not have a blueprint to work from.

So Unity gives us tools to erase negative blueprints, tools called denials. Deny the possibility of sickness, we say. Make statements like:

I do not believe in colds, weakness, inefficiency, or negativeness of any kind.

149

Or, *I deny disease as devoid of any reality and affirm health as spiritual and abiding.*

Because all of us are carrying around so many blueprints of sickness, health takes working at.

The most alive person I know is a woman. I cannot tell you her age—she refuses to accept age. But you might easily take her for half her age. She works diligently every day. She writes. She goes on strenuous lecture tours. She maintains a large house and does a great deal of the work around it—outside and in—herself. She has an active social life. Her idea of a vacation is a wilderness packtrip. A friend who accompanied her on an overseas trip confided half bitterly: "She was the only person on the tour who did not get sick." She has never had a toothache, headache, or stomachache in her life.

It may be just a coincidence, but it happens that this person who is the healthiest person I know is also the person who works hardest—has worked all her life—at developing what we in Unity call a consciousness of health. She sees herself as healthy, young, vigorous. To her, health is important. She is always affirming health. She thinks health, talks health, refuses to let thoughts of ill-health lodge in her mind. Be around her awhile and she may have you singing with her a little Unity health song like:

"I am the radiant life of God, I am, I am, I am.
I am the radiant life of God, I am, I am, I am,
The health of God, the strength of God,

Vitality, vigor, and vim of God.

I am the radiant life of God, I am, I am, I am."

Like her, we must keep the form, the shape, the vision of health before us if we would bring health forth. We must feel life surging through our thoughts, flowing through our veins. We must—as Myrtle Fillmore wrote—actually talk to the cells of our bodies and tell them how healthy they are. And we must do this not occasionally but all the time.

And what about final causes?

The final cause, Aristotle taught, *is the end, that for the sake of which, the reason why.*

If we get sick, we get sick for a reason, just as we build a house for a reason. We may not know the reason, but the reason is there. And if we are well, we are well for a reason. We are well because health is serving the purposes of our souls. We are well because the deep springs of our nature are pouring forth life and health.

Sickness and health are a response to life. When we feel faith and love, when we feel victorious and productive, our bodies are healthy. When we feel frustrated, filled with uncertainty about ourselves and life, unloved or unworthy or inadequate, we may react with sickness. I say "may" because we may also react in many other ways.

In a study made a few years ago of people who had been operated on in a certain hospital, not one was found who had not suffered a setback or a frustration. But we do not have to react to a setback or frustration by getting sick. We react in different ways. Some of these are unprofitable, like sickness. But some are profitable. Faced with having to clear a field of stones, one person may give up in exhaustion. Another may invent a machine that will help all people for all time clear the fields of stones.

This of course is what prayer is for: to help us eliminate mental and emotional factors that tend to defeat us and to build in mental and emotional factors that bring victory.

Whatever the final cause of sickness may be, the final cause of health is certain. The final cause of health is God. The final cause of health is our oneness with God.

God made us and He made us in His image and after His likeness. And God is perfect.

So the deepest urges, the deepest drives that we have are toward health. We seek to bring forth health because we are made in the image of perfection. Whatever kind of blueprint we may give the carpenter and whatever he may do with the lumber and the nails, the house he is trying to build is not the house of sickness but the house of health. The house he is trying to build is the temple of the living God.

The causes of health are physical; but the causes of health are also of the mind and soul.

The cause of health is faith. The cause of health is God. Affirm your faith in God—and health will come forth in you.

Of Freedom and Fences

Now let us take a look at freedom. Freedom! The word rings like a bell, doesn't it? It lifts the heart and stirs the passions. But just what is freedom? How free is free? How free can I be? How free can anyone be?

I have a dog, a saluki, a large, beautiful, extremely active dog. I live in a house with a large yard, almost a couple of acres. My dog has free access to the yard at all times through her own swinging door, and in house and yard she lives a very free life, for the most part doing only what she wants to do, as my wife and I make few demands on her, probably fewer than she makes on us. She flies from one end of the yard to the other, chasing anything that happens to be going by on the street, or any squirrel, cat, rabbit, or bird that ventures into the yard and she takes it into her head to chase.

My yard is fenced, but much of it is not a high fence, mainly ornamental. The fence is more a mental limit than a physical obstacle. Any time she wished she could be over it like the wind and off across the city. Not the fence, but only her own acceptance of the fence keeps her in the yard.

My dog and her fence have made me think about freedom in very different terms than I had ever thought about it before. I have come to realize that the fence does not keep her in bondage, it keeps her free!

For suppose she did jump the fence and go wandering off? Would she be free? Freer than she now is? Out in the streets is a world of laws against unleashed dogs, angry neighbors, unfriendly dogs, dogcatchers, and speeding cars. How free would she be skittering frightened and bewildered through the unfamiliar maze of the city's streets? Have you ever seen a lost dog?

In the world that lies beyond the fence, there is no way she could remain free for long; at best, she would be taken into the house of some kind person; at worst, she would be locked up in the dog pound or even run over. The fence does not limit her freedom as much as it guarantees it. It does not keep her freedom from her. On the contrary, it marks how far she can go and not lose her freedom—relative freedom, it is true, but which of us has any other kind?

What limits my dog's freedom is not that fence but the fact that she is a saluki who has to live in Lee's Summit, Missouri, U.S.A. on the continent of North America and the planet Earth. Similar limitations determine the freedom of us all.

Freedom is and always must be a relative matter. If I am wise, I do not insist on flying just because I would like to have wings. I walk when I have to. I may be free to step out of a window, but the moment I do, I lose my freedom. I lose it emphatically; I am made captive and plummeted to Earth by forces over which I have no control. I have asserted my freedom beyond my power

154

to maintain it. I have gone beyond my fence.

I built my dog's fence. In the case of human beings, they themselves may have to build their fences. Not all, of course. Many of our fences have been built by wise and loving people who lived before us, examined the world—as I have for my dog—and realized where fences were needed if they were to preserve, and not lose, their liberty. If we are wise, we accept the fences raised for us by laws, by tradition, by religious belief, by the moral code, by good manners and consideration.

For if we go too far beyond the fences of reasonable restraint, we may find we have not extended our freedom, we have lost what freedom we had. To go too far is to come up short.

I wonder if we as a nation are still here after two hundred years because the founding fathers were as aware of fences as they were of freedom when they wrote the Declaration of Independence? For they set up a very fenced-in freedom, but it was one within which they could unite to get the country started, and within which we have been able—in spite of all the persisting inequities—to be the freest people the human race has so far managed to produce.

In our time many people insist on acting as if there are no fences. "I must be free!" they assert, and they think this means they have the right to act, say, or think as they please.

You have only to think about it to see that if everyone were free to do whatever he wished to do, it would result not in freedom but in chaos. The world would become a hodgepodge, impossible work of infinite whim.

We are created to be free. The newborn child becomes enraged if you pinion him, and we never happily submit to domination, even our own. We are not puppets, no, not even God's! He made us to be free, for He made us in His image. That is why in the heart of every person stirs the desire freely to express his God-potential. That is why we feel a discontent with anything less than freedom. But we misinterpret it when we feel that it tells us to throw off every restraint, every limitation.

There are two kinds of freedom in the world. We have to be free *from* and free *to.* But sometimes we try to be free *from* what we should be free *to,* and free *to* what we should be free *from.* Then, in the name of freedom, we enslave ourselves.

For to be free means to be free *from* everything that keeps us from achieving our maximum potential; everything that weakens us; everything that tends to make us less than the most we are capable of being. And it means to be free *to* grow, to achieve dominion over our self and all the forces at work in us, to develop and express our creative powers.

The freedom that is God's free child's is not an easy freedom. It comes only with growth. It comes only with strength. It comes only with the power to stand firm and persevere. It comes only with mastery. And mastery comes only out of discipline.

Without discipline there is no freedom. My dog has helped me to learn this, too. For us to enjoy a free walk together on a country afternoon, she must have learned to heel, come, and stay when I tell her to. When she was a puppy, we both went to obedience school, and there I learned that if I were to become the master, I had first to master myself. Getting her to obey was not hard once I had learned to obey. Her discipline depended almost entirely on how disciplined I was. We are, all of us, freest when we have the maximum control over ourselves and our lives, when we can say to ourselves, "Go!" and we may go, and when we can say, "Stay!" and we stay.

The undisciplined life, the unrestrained life, is not the freest life; it is the least free. The undisciplined are imprisoned by their own lack of strength and skill. Instead of mounting on their limitations and learning to ride them to triumph, they let their limitations ride them.

The skater flying across the ice, how effortlessly she weaves through what fantastic patterns! The musician improvising at the piano, how freely her spirit ranges over the keys, fountains of music cascading from her fingertips! The basketball player, how carelessly he flicks the ball over his shoulder that it should fall so cleanly through the net! And the football player, with what unpremeditated art he spins through the field of tacklers intent on stopping him.

How free! How beautiful! we exclaim. But we know that this beautiful freedom can come only after how many months, how many years of the hardest, most persistent practice. The power to be free had to be first of all the will to submit.

Where there are no fences, there is no freedom. Not for long. Sometimes I think no one must know the meaning or the value of freedom better than the men and women in Alcoholics Anonymous. They have met their challenge and made it their conquest. They have taken the measure of their limitations and made it the measure of their freedom. They have learned how to live freely—within their fences. The peaks of freedom never have been scaled except by those who had the courage and the will to submit to the necessities of the endeavor.

"Where the Spirit of the Lord is, there is liberty." And the Spirit of the Lord is wisdom, is strength, is self-control. Even more, it is control by the highest forces and highest elements in our being.

Prayer Is a Homecoming

A Drill in the Silence

And finally, a word about prayer—not a very original word, but one that has been tested many years in Silent Unity. For almost a century we in Silent Unity have been practicing a form of prayer that we call the silence, for we know how much physical health and spiritual freedom an individual can gain from mental discipline. It is not necessary for one to go through a mind drill in order to secure God's help, but regular drill in prayer will prepare us so that with calm assurance we can unify ourselves with God and meet any need that may arise.

I believe this drill will be especially helpful to Truth students who seem to have difficulty praying. But even the advanced student will find in it a source of bodily renewal, poise, and assurance.

At the end of the drill I have included a piece that not only describes the consciousness we call the silence, but which you can use, reading it sentence by sentence, to lead you toward that consciousness.

I learned the drill that I give here from Charles Fillmore, cofounder of Unity, and May Rowland, who was the director of Silent Unity for more than fifty years. Many times through many years I have practiced this drill as they led it in Silent Unity.

Not Hard to Enter

It is not hard to enter the place of the silence. If it seems hard to us, perhaps we have been making it hard. We cannot fight our way through to God. Weeping and pleading are futile. We must let go and let God.

Some persons link the silence with occultism and look for fantastic psychic experiences from it. The purpose of the silence, however, is not to have visions or to see colored lights. Such things serve only to distract us from our true purpose, which is communion with God.

On the other hand, the silence is not a state of daydreaming or sleep. If you feel sleepy, do not try to pray unless you first can waken yourself by saying: *Awake, thou that sleepest.* The silence demands such wakefulness as is required at no other time. It is your appointment with God.

Relax

In practicing the silence you should always try to be relaxed in body and receptive in mind.

Underneath are the everlasting arms. Say this quietly. Feel the presence of God freeing you from every thought of tension. Let your whole body—every nerve, every muscle, every cell—relax and let go. Wherever you feel any tension, relax and let go. If you feel tense across your forehead, say: *Relax and let go.* If your eyes feel strained, say: *Relax and let go.* If you are tense in any other part of your body, say: *Relax and let go,* until from the top of your head to the soles of your feet you are perfectly relaxed. This concludes the first step in the drill.

Be Still

Be still, and know that I am God. Say this silently. Repeat it until the words take on new meaning, a living meaning, and you feel the stillness deep down inside with your whole mind, your whole being.

This is the second step in the practice of the silence, and it is perhaps the most important of all. Only in stillness can you unify yourself with God, only when thoughts and feelings are quieted and the doors of the senses are shut. Not through our human powers and understanding do we attain our good, but through letting go of doubts and limiting personal claims and turning to God.

Be still, and know that I am God. Know it. Know it now. You are comfortable, relaxed, still. You are in the presence of God.

Turn your attention now to the top of your head and say silently or aloud, as you wish: *I am the light of the world.*

Using Affirmations

In the practice of the silence you will find it wise to

use affirmations, for they will help you to direct and to control your thoughts. But there is a surer speech than that of syllables, a higher communion than that of words. God hears your inmost thoughts. Your faith and love speak for you. Your faith and love unify you with Him, make your mind His mind, your body His body, your spirit His Spirit, your life His life, your will His will.

You do not have to cajole or coerce God; His love has already encompassed the fulfillment of your needs. It is only you whom your prayers have to change. Use affirmations to direct your thoughts, to make them clear, sharp, pointed; then be still and listen. It is God's voice that you wish to hear.

Light

I am the light of the world. Declare this. Then be still until you actually feel the light of Spirit through you and over you, until you feel yourself immersed as in a sea of light, your whole being illumined, awake, exalted, the "light of the world."

Now, center your attention just above the eyes and declare: *I am divine intelligence.*

Emerson said: *The only real prosperity that I can have is a rush of ideas.* Divine Mind is a reservoir of ideas, good ideas, yours to draw on, yours to use. No sluggishness, physical or mental, no doubt or fear can remain in you, for you have opened your mind to the inspiration of God. You are alive, awake, alert, joyous, healthy, and enthusiastic. You are divine intelligence.

Now, center your attention at the eyes and say: *I see with the eyes of Spirit.*

Your eyes are the watchful servants of a mind that sees only the perfection of Spirit. All sense of tension or fatigue is dropping away from your eyes before the inflow of divine energy. They are strong, clear-seeing eyes. Your spiritual vision, too, is renewed. You see truth more clearly. You see with the eyes of Spirit.

Power

Centering your attention at the throat, affirm: *All power is given unto me in mind and body.*

The power of God is working through you to free you from every negative influence. Nothing can hold you in bondage. You are the overcomer, a child of God. All power is yours to control your thoughts, to vitalize your body, to gain success, to bless others. Unleash your spiritual forces. All power is given unto you in mind and body.

Freedom

Now, fix your thought at the back of your neck and say: *I am unfettered and unbound.*

You are free with the freedom of Spirit. No false condition has any power over you. You are in truth a child of the living God. Poised in the consciousness of your Christ mastery, you are unfettered and unbound.

Strength

Now, directing your attention toward your back, declare: *I am strong in the Lord and in the power of His might.*

Your yoke is easy, and your burden is light. The strength of the Lord is pouring through your spinal column, strengthening nerve and bone. No longer bowed by burdens—your own, your family's, or the world's—your back is straight and sturdy. Free, poised, lighthearted, you face life confidently, strong in the Lord and in the power of His might.

Love

Turn your thought toward your heart and declare: *I am the expression of divine love.*

Love transforms. Love transfigures. Love fills the heart with harmony. Love fills the mind with kind, helpful thoughts. Love fills the lips with words of praise and cheer. Love fills life, fills it to overflowing with happiness and peace. Whatever the need or problem, divine love is the answer.

Substance

Now, fix your attention at the pit of the stomach and say: *I am satisfied with divine substance.*

The substance of God erases fatigue from your body, renews tissues, replenishes energy. It stabilizes your mind. It prospers your affairs. Every longing of your heart, every need of your life is fulfilled. You are satisfied with divine substance.

Order

When you have gained a full realization of substance, focus your attention at the navel and realize: *Divine order is established in my mind and body.*

The law is unchanging, absolute. Now you are in harmony with this law. It governs and guides you. It is active in your mind, harmonizing your thoughts. It is active in your body, adjusting its functions. It is active in your affairs, establishing peace, success, and joy. Divine order is established in your mind and body.

Life

Now, center your thoughts at the lower part of the abdomen and say: *I am alive forevermore in Christ Jesus.*

You have entered the secret place of life. Life charges your mind, flows through your veins, permeates your tissues, every nerve, every muscle, every cell. Your eyes shine, your skin glows, your faculties are sharpened, your whole body radiates health. You are one with life, the Christ life, ever-renewing life. You are alive forevermore in Christ Jesus.

Finally, centering your thought in your feet and legs, affirm: *I walk in paths of righteousness and peace.*

The strength and swiftness of God enter into your feet and legs so that your way is made easy. The light of His intelligence shines around you so that your way is made plain. His Spirit goes before you so that your way is made successful. God's way for you is joyous, a way of safety and security. You walk in paths of righteousness and peace.

Oneness with God

If you have faithfully followed all the steps of this drill in the silence, you are now fully aware of your oneness with God. From the top of your head to the soles of your feet you feel His tingling life. Your mind is charged with His power. Your heart is lifted up by His love. Your whole being is filled with a new sense of peace and satisfaction. You can affirm in the knowledge that it is true: *I am a child of the living God.*

Now out of the stillness comes the "still small voice," not a human voice, speaking in your native tongue, but the voice of God, which speaks as an inner knowing, a strong conviction, and carries to the listening heart the assurance that all is well.

Fulfillment

Ask, and it shall be given you; seek, and ye shall find; knock, and it shall be opened unto you. You have asked, and the Father's good is freely proffered. You have sought, and the way to perfection is revealed. You have knocked, and the doors of the kingdom are open. Fulfillment is yours. The power to bless others is yours. Receive and rejoice!

The Place of Peace

Have you ever been in a garden in the evening? The honey-heavy bees are home from the clover. The moths suck the sweetness of the moonflowers. The wind does not stir among the drooping leaves. Over every leaf and flower peace broods like a bird, and like a bird peace broods over the heart.

Have you ever walked alone through falling snow at night? Like a mantle it wraps you away from the familiar world of things and people, claims and cares. It wipes away the ugliness and scars of every day and makes all things one in white simplicity. The snow is a solitude of silence.

Truly "silence is the element in which great things fashion themselves together."

There are many kinds of silence.

There is the drowsy silence of the noonday fields. There is the restless silence of the sleeping city. There is the silence of the grief too deep for tears and of the joy too full for laughter. There is the understanding silence that falls between new lovers and old friends. The movement of the heavens, the growth of living things are silent. There is the silence of human thought.

But deeper is the silence of the place of peace within you. Deeper is the silence where you commune with God.

Here workaday worries fade away. When you go into the place of the silence, you leave outside the dusty cares of every day, as an Oriental leaves his shoes outside his holy place of prayer.

This is a holy place, a place to which you can turn for rest and release from fear and care. Stillness fills it. The peace of God is in it. Here your mind becomes as a little child's, lovely and true and pure. Here your thought is stayed on the things that are good and just and merciful. When you enter here, the world outside and all your troubles drop away, and you rise at last body stilled, mind stilled, refreshed, and restored.

This place is not far away or difficult of access. It is right where you are now. It is right where you are whenever you shut the doors of the senses, still the importuning of little thoughts, and go alone with God. It is the place of the silence.

In the place of the silence there are stillness and peace. It is not the stillness of sleep. It is not the peace of dreams. It is such stillness as the tree must know when in the summer afternoon its outstretched leaves soak in the sun. It is such peace as the bird must know when with no movement of its wings it floats serene upon the moving air. It is the stillness of God's sustaining presence, the peace of His all-infolding life.

The silence is a windless place of thought in which the mind may walk alone and find rest. The silence is a deep pool in which the soul may gaze into the depths of itself. The silence is a bridge from you to God.

Is not music more beautiful because there are rests? Is not eloquence more passionate when it has pauses? How much lovelier than the loveliest song is the unheard music in your heart! How much deeper than the most passionate outpouring are your unuttered feelings! The silence is the speech that transcends speech, the conversation of your soul with God, wordless and wonderful.

It is in silence that God writes on the emptiness of space and punctuates His sentences with stars. It is in silence that great thoughts are born. It is in silence that our lives are fashioned and find meaning.

Homecoming after a journey—what is better than that? And what is better after the tumult of the world than to turn to God?

Have you ever welcomed home someone you love who had been away a long time? In the midst of the turmoil, the jostling elbows, the indifferent voices, the hurrying feet, when the one you love came through the gate, for a moment the noise and confusion faded away, you reached out your hands and your heart, and there were only love and peace and joy. So when you go into the place of the silence, no matter what the outer world may hold, for a moment the noise and confusion fade away, and in the presence of the One you love, the One who loves you, there are only peace and joy.

In the very center of silence is the presence of God. What is the presence of God? It is not sound or sight or even thought. It is the strength you are in need of. It is the courage you did not have before. It is the inspiration you are seeking. It is the love that tells you you are not alone. It is the assurance that all is well, like a light from a window on a lonely road at night, like the hand of a friend stretched out in a moment of need, like the sight of your own home after a weary journey.

In the silence you come home to God. Through the meadows of the mind, in the valley of content, by the pools of renewal, in the place of the silence, there you walk and talk with Him.

In the silence is strength for the tired body. In the silence is light for the joyless mind. In the silence is love for the lonely spirit. In the silence is peace for the troubled heart. There workaday worries fade away. There the whole being becomes a place of prayer, a holy temple set upon a hill. There God becomes a living presence. There you become His child.

And you "shall have some peace there, for peace comes
    dropping slow,
Dropping from the veils of the morning to where the
    cricket sings;
There midnight's all a glimmer, and noon a purple
    glow,
And evening full of the linnet's wings."

Hymn ... for a Sunrise Service

Out of earth, shapeless; out of air, invisible; out of water, colorless; out of fire, too insubstantial to be weighed—the master Maker of all that is made wills into being His world of shapes, colors, motions, creatures, things.

O You who made all that is made, I pray You that You make me like the earth.

Give me earth's power to bring life out of death!

From time's beginning, all things have died and fallen into the earth. Yet the earth is not a tomb, but a womb. It was a handful of earth God took for the making of us human beings.

O the teeming, fruitful earth, the productive earth! I too would be productive. I would bring forth living thoughts as the earth brings forth living forms, original, useful, beautiful. I would make things beautiful as earth makes things beautiful. All seasons and all places, earth makes beautiful.

Earth knows that everything will pass and that change is natural. Through day and night, winter and summer, the earth turns patiently.

Earth does not ask if anyone who plants a seed is good or bad. Earth accepts.

Earth has a power for strength and repose. Those

who are close to earth have tranquil minds.

Jesus was close to earth. He loved to be alone in deserts and on mountains. He spoke of sowing and reaping, of vineyards and fruit trees and flocks, and of the lilies of the field.

John called Him the Lamb of God. When He thought of how we might remember Him, He took up bread and wine.

O You who made all that is made, I pray You that You make me like air.

The blue enveloping air! world of winds and clouds! It cannot be contained; it spills over everywhere. I feel its lift, whose only wings are thoughts. O the spring of the air! It can be pressed down, but it flies back with greater force.

With easy grace it sweeps a mountain crest in storm, ripples the surface of a lake, or stirs a single leaf on the poplar tree in my garden.

It goes about invisibly to do its works, doing them because its nature is to do them, not for praise.

And how freely air gives itself to all! It never withholds, rushes to fill any emptiness. Yet it is never used up.

Nothing is more responsive to change than air, yet nothing remains more the same.

This air I breathe, Moses breathed, Socrates breathed, Jesus breathed. All living things have breathed it from the beginning of time. Yet it is still the breath of life.

O You who made all that is made, I pray You that You make me like water.

In me are tides no less than in the sea. I would have a mind and spirit like water.

Water never resists, yet it wears away the most resistant things.

Water fits itself to conditions, takes the shape of any bowl it is poured into. Yet nothing shapes more things than water; the continents have the shape it gives them.

Water does work, but is never busy. It may turn a mill or light a city, but not by trying. Water lets itself be used.

Water has learned humility. It is colorless, yet what is a rainbow but water? It is tasteless, yet what is there better to drink? It always seeks the lowest place. But those in high places come to drink of it.

Jesus loved to walk by water. He went to it not only to quench His thirst, but for peace.

O You who made all that is made, I pray You that You make me like fire.

Dance and sing, my spirits, like fire.

Imagination, soar like fire.

Thoughts, give light as fire gives light.

Heart, be warm as fire is warm.

Words, give cheer as fire gives cheer.

Let me be as a refiner's fire. Let the dross be burned away so that any gold that may be there will shine forth.

Fire changes what it touches. From the dry fagots of accustomed thought, let what I write strike light, strike beauty, strike the warmth of love, strike the fire of God.

I would burn with the fire that fell from heaven and leapt as tongues of flame around the heads of the apostles on the day of Pentecost and loosed their tongues so that they babbled as if drunk of mysteries and truths.

O You who made all that is made, I pray You that You make me like Yourself.

You are the changeless, always changing; the eternal, momently fulfilled; the formless, only glimpsed in forms. You are freedom, yet the order that is indispensable to freedom; law, yet the love that is beyond law; power, yet the peace that is at the center of power.

O Mind of God, what must the mind be like that thinks suns, porpoises, trees, grasshoppers, moonflowers, comets, rocks, streams, sunsets, human beings!

O Heart of God, what must the heart be like that

circles with its love the unimaginable reaches of the world of space, yet feels a sparrow's fall!

How great You are, O God; how little I seem to be, that we should feel so near!

But You have made Yourself the Son of man. You are in us all no less than in Him who said: *Inasmuch as ye have done* it *unto one of the least of these my brethren, ye have done* it *unto me.*

God, You are mind. You have given me the power of thought.

You are substance. You have given me a body.

You are love. You have given me a heart to love.

You are life. You have given me existence.

You are spirit. You have given me the passion to perfect.

As a grain of dust is the earth, and a breath of air the atmosphere, and a raindrop the waters of the firmament, and a candleflame the quintessence of light and fire—so You are in me and I am in You.

You are spirit, but You have made Yourself flesh.

And in this flesh, where fire and water, earth and air commingle and are one, I would be one with You.

Today Is Forever, Forever Today

Since I began this book with a piece about time, now time brings it to an end, for this last piece is also about time. I hope you don't think I have taken an eternity to get here.

When Ignatius Loyola, who founded the Jesuits, was a young student, he was playing a game of ball one afternoon with some of his friends when they got to discussing what they would do if they suddenly found out the world was going to end the next day.

Half of Ignatius' friends declared that they would rush to find a wine cask and the comforting arms of a lover. The other half declared that they would rush to a church and cast themselves on their knees in prayer.

But Ignatius simply said, "I would keep on playing my game."

I have always thought Ignatius had exactly the right attitude toward time.

Half of Ignatius' friends thought that all they had was today and they had better grab everything it had to give before it was lost to them forever. The other half thought that all that counts is forever and they had better spend today preparing for it.

But Ignatius knew that life is not just for today or just for forever, but for both; and you cannot make the most of either one without considering it in the context of the other.

If you live as if all you have is today, you will flit from moment to moment across the surface of things.

If you live as if all that counts is forever, you will forever postpone living.

To live fully, you have to live today as if you have all forever, and live forever as if all you have is today.

Time comes to us a moment at a time.

We either use it or lose it.

To have the full-time use of time, this then is how we have to live:

We have to live today as if we had all forever, and live forever as if all we had was today.

I do not believe you will ever find any insight more important to you than this. The people who go about singing, "It's later than you think," are mistaken. So was the poet Browning when he wrote, "What's time? leave Now for dogs and apes! Man has Forever."

It is not enough to live for forever.

It is not enough to live for today.

We have to live for both—and both at the same time.

The world itself is arranged to show us this. There is day but there is also night. There is waking but there is also sleep. When we do not give part of our day to sleep, what a dreary day it becomes. But what a weary day it would be if we gave it all to sleep.

Dreams and sleeping must give way to waking, and waking to dreams and sleep. If today would be lived as part of forever, forever can only be lived in terms of to-day.

Eternity is like the moon that keeps only one face toward us always, and the face that eternity keeps toward us is today's.

The amazing thing is that we all come into life with the right attitude toward time. Watch a child. He lives wholly in the moment—not as if this were all the time he had, but as if he had all the time in the world. He does not grasp the moment as it flies past, fearful lest it elude him; he takes it on the wing and flies with it.

Is he examining a colored pebble he has picked up in the street? Galileo gazing for the first time at the moons of Jupiter through his newly invented telescope was no more absorbed.

To a child, now is an eternity, and eternity is nothing but now.

A child has forever to do the least thing in, but a moment longer than a moment is too long to wait.

Time is the stuff we make a life out of. Time is not life, but we make life out of it. How we handle it, the attitude we take toward it, determines to a great extent what we make out of our lives.

Too often when we become concerned about time and begin to think of getting the most out of it, it is because we feel that it is slipping away and we had better grab it quickly. But this is to live by only half our equation—to live as if all we have is today—and therefore to live half a life.

The moment never puts down very deep roots. The moment is on the move. And when we live for the moment, we live on the move; we are always in a hurry. We live as if we were renters only—and this may be, but we need the property owner's viewpoint. For it is not often when we rent that we take much care of the property or make many improvements; we do not plant many trees. When we live fully, we plant trees, even when we know we may never sit beneath their shade.

Most of us have to learn to live today, for most of us put off our good. Putting off happiness is the world's most wasteful habit. And it is a habit. The more we do it, the more it grows. We start putting off the things we do not want to have, but we end putting off even the things we want to have.

Some people live in a constant tomorrow. Even their pleasures, they postpone. If they have a task, some later time is always soon enough to start to think about it.

Perhaps we are all like this. Someday we will . . . read that book, see that show, call that friend, take that walk in the woods, go to that restaurant, make that trip . . . some day!

Like Saint Augustine when he felt God tugging at his soul to make something more out of his life, we cry out, "Presently, Lord—presently."

Once we have formed the habit of looking for our happiness in the future, that is where we are always looking for it. It has been said that most people merely endure the present, waiting for the future—but that's a long, long wait.

The wife of a friend of mine became ill. A doctor told them she had no chance to recover.

She took the blow in stride and went on living as positively and energetically and happily as she was able; she kept working at what she had to work at. She kept on enjoying what there was to enjoy. When unpleasant moments came, she met them as well as she could and then went back to her work or play or rest or whatever was there.

But for my friend, the fear of what was going to happen kept him from putting himself into what was happening, and life became a weary round of waiting for the end.

One morning his wife took him in her arms and said to him, "We are alive today.

"Tomorrow anything may happen—to anyone. A rich uncle may leave us a million dollars. The Earth may collide with a comet. What tomorrow may bring, neither of us knows.

"But we do know that we are alive today. Today is all anyone has—a newborn baby, an old, old man—no more, no less.

"This doesn't mean we should live as if this were our last day. This is what you have been doing. First day, last day—this does not matter. We are alive today. Today is the time we have. If you can think of a better way to live it, let's do it. Not because it's about to end, but because it's the time we have and we should live it as fully as we can.

183

"Here we are today, having one another, loving one another, just as much as we ever have, more perhaps. And just as much alive as we ever have been, in many ways more.

"We are alive today."

Suddenly he saw that to put off living today because of what tomorrow may bring is to put off living forever, and this is true whether we put it off out of dread or out of anticipation.

Jesus said: *"Do not be anxious about tomorrow, for tomorrow will be anxious for itself. Let the day's own trouble be sufficient for the day."*—(Matt. 6:34 RSV)

It is just as much a waste of time to wait for our ships to come in as it is to look for them to founder. Either habit of thought keeps us from living the life that is ours now.

We live moment by moment, but we live the moment in the context of eternity. We may be doing a great thing; we may be doing a little thing; we may be doing nothing. Great thing, little thing, nothing—each alone and all altogether, they may be making for the maximum life.

To get the full-time use of time, you have to get the most out of passing everyday events as you do out of great and memorable ones. Life is made up mainly of little things.

Once there was a little saint who had lived a long and holy and happy life, so one day God sent His angel to bring him to the abode of eternity. The angel found the little saint in the kitchen, washing the pots and pans.

"The time has come," said the angel, "for you to take up your abode in eternity. God has sent me to bring you to Him."

"I thank God for thinking of me," said the little saint, "but as you can see, there is this great heap of pots and pans to be washed as well as quite a few other things that need doing to set this kitchen in order. I don't want to seem ungrateful, but do you think I might put off taking up my abode in eternity until I have finished this?"

The angel looked at him in the wise and loving way of angels. "I'll see what can be arranged," he said and vanished.

The little saint went on with his pots and pans and the few other things that needed doing in the kitchen and a great number of other things besides that.

One day as he stood hoeing in the garden, there again was the angel. The saint shrugged his shoulders as if to say, "I'm sorry about this," and pointed with his hoe up and down the garden rows.

"Look at all these weeds," he said. "You can see for yourself all the things that need to be done in this garden. There are corn and beans to be planted and a row of marigolds along the fence there, and the cold frame needs to be rebuilt. Do you think eternity can hold off a little longer?"

The angel looked at the saint and smiled, and again he vanished.

185

So the saint went on hoeing the garden, and after he had hoed the garden, he painted the barn, and after he had painted the barn, he had the poor to visit.

What with one thing and another, time raced ahead until one day he was in the hospital tending the sick. He had just finished giving a drink of cold water to a feverish patient when he looked up and there was the angel once more.

This time the saint said nothing. He just spread his hands in a gesture of resignation and compassion and drew the angel's eyes after his own around the hospital ward where all the many sufferers were waiting for him to tend to them. Without a word the angel vanished.

That evening when the little saint went back to the monastery, he ate his simple meal with his fellow monks and afterward sat with a couple of his cronies for a while swapping stories. But when he had gone to his cell and sunk down on his pallet, he began to think about the angel and how he had put him off for such a long time. It had been a very busy day and suddenly he felt very old and very tired, and he said, "God, if You would like to send Your angel again, I think I would like to see him now."

He had no sooner spoken than the angel stood beside him.

"If you still want to take me," said the saint, "I am ready to go with you now to take up my abode in eternity."

The angel looked at the little saint in the wise and

loving way angels look, and he smiled a warm, soft smile.

"Where do you think you have been?" he said.

154-F-7936-10M-8-85